Gia Scala:
The First Gia....

A memoir narrated by her sister Tina,

Written and researched by Sterling Saint James

Author: Sterling Saint James

Copyright © S.S.J. Trust

ISBN: 978-0-9893695-1-0

"Gia Scala" painting located on back cover upper right hand, by Tom Smith,
Vancouver, British Columbia

Published by Parhelion House

Parhelion House, Publisher
info@ParhelionHouse.com

Table of Contents

Unbelievable...5

The Death Certificate 19

Messina, Sicily 23

Nazi Invasion & Allied Response.......................51

Reconnecting 71

Ireland 75

Our Return to Messina....................................93

Good-Bye Gia 101

Hello Breasts..107

Gia & her King of Cool 129

The Hollywood Image 139

Gia Meets Clint Eastwood...............................149

In Like Flynn 161

1957 ... a Pivotal Year 180

Through Difficult Times.................................206

The Bridge...214

The Hollywood Hookup..................................223

The Wedding & Reception Photo Album 231

A Marriage in Haste? 241

The Guns of Navarone...................................252

A New Robin in the Hood 261

It's Me, Tina! 267

Rear Ended! 283

Alone 286

Gia... Not Herself 297

Sadly a Short Life 304

The Funeral 311

To Live One Day as a Lion.... 320

Tina's Photo Album 323

Filmography 342

Index 346

Unbelievable

Four decades ago my sister Gia Scala was discovered dead in her Hollywood Hills home. Because of her movie star fame, and how she was found with bottles of alcohol and a vial missing only three tablets of her prescription for Valium along side her bed, the Police and the media jumped to the conclusion she committed suicide. That salacious story blasted over the television news, radio, and in newspapers. Recklessly, without due diligence, the media besmirched her reputation. Later, in a second page story, the narrative was slightly tweaked as an accidental overdose of drugs and alcohol instead of suicide. But, the shocking news of a beautiful movie star taking her life has tainted Gia's reputation irrevocably.

It was odd that the Los Angeles Coroner amended her Death Certificate two times. After the autopsy, the official cause of death became acute ethanol and barbiturate intoxication added to that diffuse nonspecific myocardiopathy.

However, when I spoke to the Los Angeles County pathologist David Katsuyama who had worked on the case, he commented, "There was so little oxygen flowing to her brain … that it's a wonder your sister could think at all." He told me that he discovered she had an advanced stage of arteriole sclerosis, and premature dementia.

At that I was confused because I had spoken to her before her death and she was fine. Recently returned from Paris where she had resided for a time in a borrowed apartment, it was her friend and neighbor Henry Miller's second home. He was not using it when he lent it to her.

In Paris she studied the art of cooking at the Cordon Bleu Cooking School, and took classes in fine art painting. Excited to begin a new career as a painter, she had collected art for years and became friends with artists one of whom was Paulo or Paul Picasso, Pablo's first son with his wife Olga Khokhlova, the Russian ballet dancer. What the lab tech told me was so out of character for Gia that I thought perhaps he wasn't looking at Gia's brain, perhaps, not even her body! .

I remember the Police strung yellow tape around her home and called it a crime scene; I was not allowed to enter. After the criminal investigation, the Police determined that there was no homicide; the crime scene was closed. I then entered her home and went up stairs to her bedroom; the place the Police had told me Gia's body was found. I saw blood on her pillow and on the floor next to her bed was an arrangement of bottles of alcohol, drinking glasses, and small empty vial of prescription Valium; the scene was too perfectly set-up, like movie studio staging. But the strangest thing was during the time between the Police closed the crime scene and I was able to enter her home, in that short interval of a couple of days, her home had been broken into. I discovered some pieces of furniture missing, her desk drawers were open, papers rifled through and scattered about. Someone was looking for something. I became suspicious and I asked the Police about this; they told me to hire a private investigator.

I started to look into the situation because what kept me motivated was the death scene; it seemed artificial, out of character for Gia. What I meant she was an organized person; she would not have bottles and her prescription strewn about her bedroom. And she was an attractive woman who took pride in her looks.

I think most women who anticipate suicide want to be found beautiful, especially Gia the movie star. With make-up on, her haired coiffed, dressed in a sexy negligee, lying perfectly on satin sheets. But, she was found nude, sprawled out over her bed with bruises on her body, blood on her pillow, and the front door to her home was left open!

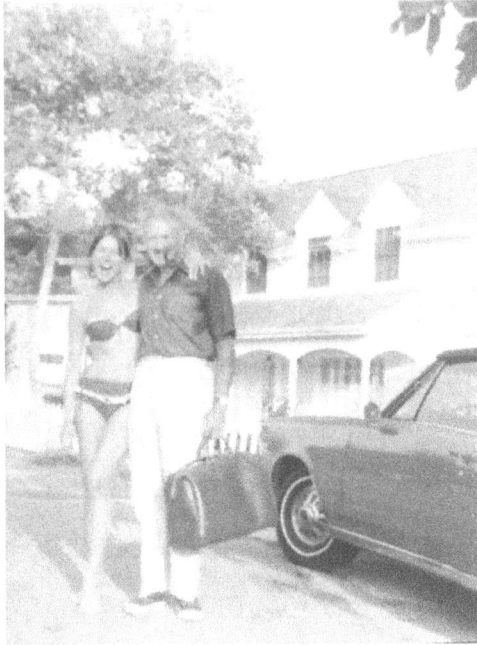

Above: Gia in front of her home on Woodrow Wilson Drive, in Hollywood. Her athletic body shows no signs of alcohol indulgence or drug use. Gia is standing next to the actor Anthony Quayle, who also appeared in the film "The Guns of Navarone."

When I read the Police report, it said that 21 year old Daniel La Biena on or about six o'clock p.m. on April 30, 1972 discovered the front door to her home open. At that he walked in, went upstairs and found Gia in bed. When he went to wake her, she was dead. But, earlier that day, at eight o'clock in the morning, Gia called the Police on La Biena, his friend Larry Langston, and two others. They were struggling musicians who did odd jobs in the neighborhood such as lawn maintenance. When Daniel moved into Gia's extra room above her garage, he invited his buddies also to move into the room. She didn't like that at all, but she was a kind-hearted person, she allowed them to stay temporarily. However, when something must have went wrong, she had to call the Police to have them removed from her home. When I learned this, I became suspicious, why would La Biena return to Gia's home after the Police asked him to leave earlier that day? When he was asked that question, he told the Police he returned so he could thank Gia for her hospitality.

Later when I was paying her household bills, on the phone bill I saw there was a call made from Gia's home on the day of her death around midnight. At that time, she had been dead six hours. The phone call was made to Long Beach, California. When I called that number and a woman answered, she did not speak English, and I do not speak Spanish. But, the hour that the phone call was made indicated that someone was in Gia's home after she had died, when the Police still had the home roped off with yellow crime tape.

When I began straightened up her desk, that was when I discovered papers whereby she made Guy Williams, the actor, and her ex-husband's best friend, the beneficiary of her Screen Actor's Guild death benefits. That seemed odd because she did not make a will; she had no directives as what to do with her possessions if she passed. Obviously she had not been anticipating dying at thirty-eight years old, but she took care of Guy. Why? What was her motive?

Above: Henry Miller & Gia. Miller was a fine arts enthusiast, who collected art & was a painter in his own right. This photograph was taken at Miller's home in Pacific Palisades, California.

Gia was intelligent and possessed a deep innate sense of psychology. In school her nickname was the Little Philosopher. When we were girls, I watched her talk to Father, he could never say no to what ever she wanted. She knew what to say to get what she wanted. Then I thought about Guy, that she nominated him to be the beneficiary of her death benefits. What was she implying with this? Was it for Guy? Or was she indirectly speaking to her ex husband? Of course, her divorce devastated her. When her ex left her to live with Rock Hudson, I can imagine she felt betrayed. She entered into her marriage in good faith, but did he?

I saw a bill for her safe-deposit box, but where was the key? During probate, I went to the bank with the Los Angeles County District Attorney to open the box. A bank employee drilled the lock on the box. When it was opened, there was nothing in it. What happened to her jewelry, where was her wedding ring?

Later I found her divorce documents. That was the first time I had read them. I saw where her ex agreed to give her one thousand dollars a month alimony for ten years, in present day money that would be close to five thousand dollars a month. How could he afford it? Although he had had a part in the television series "Northwest Passage," but when the series ended, he became a struggling actor who later decided to leave show business and become an investment banker. The document read that upon his death or her death, the alimony payments were extinguished.

I began to put the pieces together and along with the terrible press that created an image of her as a drugged out drunk, I started to consider the terrible idea that her death possibly was not accidental. My beautiful, smart, and talented sister, whom I loved, was killed.

I became depressed because she had passed, but the possibility that she could have been killed was overwhelming. Heart brokenly sad, my world shrunk around me. The shock of her death, the breaking and entering of her home, things missing, safe deposit box empty; I gathered my strength, and miserably I went forward.

I needed to get things in order. First, I had to sell her home because to be in the house where she was killed was awful; second, there was a large mortgage on it that had to be paid each month. I didn't want the bank to foreclose on my sister's home. There was no money in Gia's bank account. I remember the day I went to her bank and spoke to the manager. He told me that a day or so before she died, she withdrew a great deal of money. He was hesitant to give it to her because she was with three hippie type guys. Suspicious, but it was her money and she had the right to take it out no matter who accompanied her to the bank.

Where was that money? It was not in her home, it was not in her safe-deposit box, I had gone through her possessions, private papers, and there was no money.

I was getting the home ready to sell; I sold the furniture, and given some away, I had taken her papers and possessions to my apartment. Nothing was left but two beds: one in her bedroom and one in the second bedroom. One day

I went to check on the home, I walked up the stairs, opened her bedroom door, and saw something on the bed. When I looked closer it was a book, a large black book. The title read: "Your Days Are Numbered!"

This was not my book; I had never seen it before. Someone had to have entered the home and put it on the bed. Was this a message for me? If it was what did it mean? Was I next?

I started shaking; it felt like my knees were going to give out. Who had the key to the house, or did someone break in again? There was nothing left in the house to steal, so this book placed on Gia's bed was meant for me. Why would someone want to hurt me? Then I thought, maybe I'm asking too many questions about Gia's death. I got out of there as quick as I could; I got into my car and went home to my apartment. I never went back to that house again. I called a realtor, her name was Elaine Young, she was the ex-wife of the actor Gig Young. Gia had worked in a movie with Gig. I asked her to list the house, and she did.

The actress Sally Kellerman bought Gia's home for what I can remember about seventy thousand dollars. Sally was familiar with the home because when Gia went to Paris, she had rented the house to Sally. Upon returning home and moving back in, Gia discovered that Sally had painted all the interior walls in the home black. After Gia's death, when I was anticipating selling, I thought that the house wouldn't sell with black walls. I had the walls painted a soft shade of yellow.

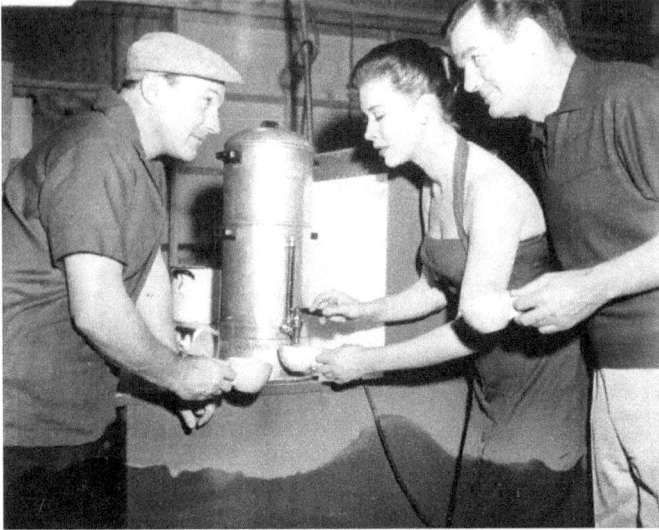

Above: L. to R.: Gene Kelly, the director, Gia Scala, Gig Young, taking a coffee break while filming "The Tunnel of Love."

I was glad when Gia's home sold because it was a closure for me. The end of my beautiful sister who came to the United States with so much hope, the end of a wonderful spirit who will continue on in celluloid into perpetuity.

For me, although physically she is no more, she remains alive in my memories. I remember her as a charismatic individual who loved life, and drama. At times she could be melodramatic, stealing the attention with a glance, a gesture, yet without a word spoken. It was that thin line between reality and Hollywood --a tightrope walker's nightmare, but for her it was the challenge, the daringness of will she be caught? Or will she get away with it? From my earliest memories of Gia, she defied the social customs, and society's rules: a true rebel, not the James Dean type, but demurely she taunted that imaginary line.

Hollywood adored her, her star rose quickly. She once said to me that if stardom would have been a struggle, she would have enjoyed it more, for the challenge. Admired and successful, her numerous movie, and television credits, along with the society she moved in of writers, painters, and actors, she lived in a world that loved her, and she enjoyed her life as an artist and an actress, she was on the creative edge.

Known as one of the most stunningly beautiful women in Hollywood, although naturally a dirty-dishwater blond, the Hollywood studios exploited her Italian exoticness and changed her hair color to dark brown. This enhanced her Mediterranean turquoise – blue eyes. With her five foot eight inch height and shapely body, she moved gracefully like an haute contour fashion model. Smoothly gliding her way down the red carpet; she knew what to wear with bewitching elegance, a *fashionista* ahead of times.

Most people did not know that she was a tremendous athlete: she loved tennis, swimming, and horseback riding. Fearless and competitive to the extent that led her to be reckless, so much so that she "pushed the envelop" into the extreme, but it was just that --her daring style along with her physical beauty made her an indelible personality.

However, beauty can be a double edged sword: the old adage comes to mind, "The beautiful woman desires the luck of the plain one." Men buzzed around Gia. Some caught her attention such as Steve McQueen. A charismatic person, but it was not meant to be. She met Don Burnett, a devilishly handsome actor who could hypnotize with his sharp blue eyes; Gia became smitten. She married him with adore and lust, he, on the other hand, was a cool number.

After the marriage, she put her career on hold in order to become his perfect wife; he used her fame and connections to help his struggling acting career, and spent her money.

Why then was her life cut short? Who was to gain by her death? I've been asking these questions for more than forty years. I offer to you my impressions of my sister Gia from my earliest memories of her to the last. Perhaps you will be able to recognize what put into motion my sister's fate.

Tina Scala
December 2014

Tina Scala

July 16, 1936, Milli San Marco, Sicily
January 10, 2022, Las Vegas, Nevada

Gia near Gmunden, Austria, 1960

The Death Certificate

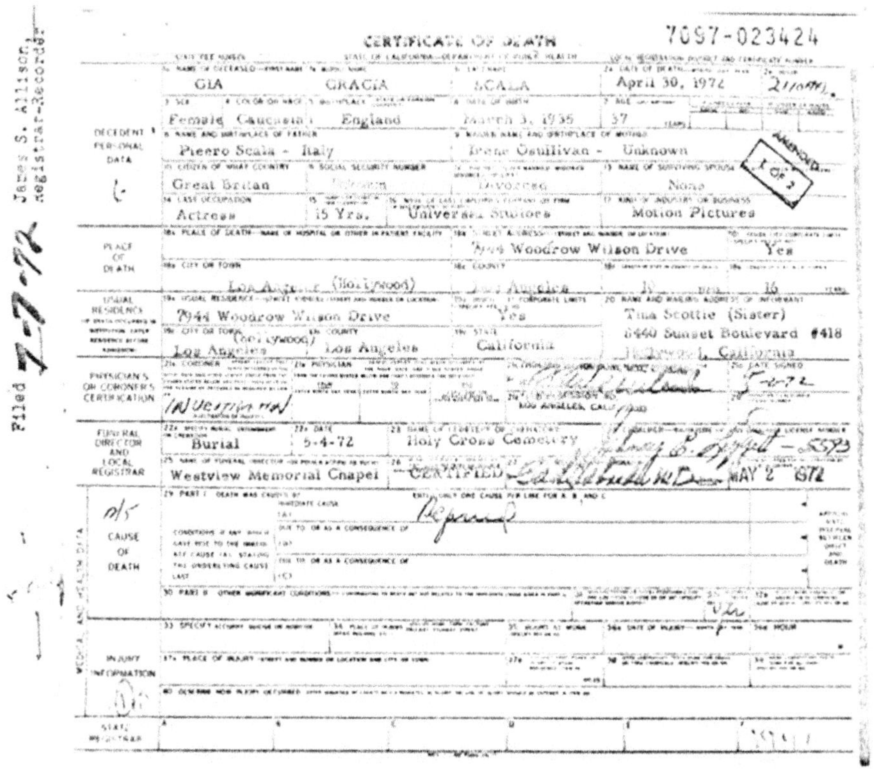

Beautiful Gia

I was at my apartment that evening. Close to ten o'clock when Stan Adams, a photographer, knocked at my door. He had brought the contact prints of the photo session that I had posed for the previous day; they were the photos that I was planning to use in my modeling portfolio

I remember when Stan came into my apartment, he saw my Chess set on the table and asked, "Do you play Chess?" I told him that I was learning and that I had bought Bobby Fischer's book. We were making small talk, commenting on the photos. I could hear my television on in the background, but I wasn't paying attention to it. I remember looking at the contact photos under a loop when the ten o'clock news began with: Actress Gia Scala found dead this evening at home; details after the break.

I said, "No! This is not true!" Immediately, I called Gia on the phone. A man who identified himself as a Police Officer answered. I can't remember what he said because I was in a panic, terrified at the thought that my sister was dead. I was shaking, dazed, and just out of my mind. I could not calm down. Stan became concerned. He called a doctor friend of his. When the doctor arrived and saw my condition, he gave me a sedative, and helped me to bed. I remember sinking into sleep thinking about my big sister: how beautiful she was, so smart, I adored her, she was my idol, I didn't know what to do next, how I could go on without her, my older sister although at times domineering, she knew how to control me, she was more like a mother than a sister. I loved her, I idolized her. I began thinking about when I was a girl living in our home in Messina with Mother, Father, Grandfather and …Gia.

CB

Gia, on a train in Germany, 1960

Messina, Sicily

One of my first memories of Gia was spying on her through the keyhole of our living room door; I watched her playing tea party with some of her little friends who came to visit. She wouldn't let me join the fun because she said that I wasn't old enough. I was the six year old baby sister, when she was all of eight. But her objections to my youth did not stop me from spying on her through the keyhole.

I saw them laughing and giggling as Gia poured more tea. Sometimes Mother came to check up on them, and when I heard her come down the hallway, I'd run on tip-toes back to my bedroom, close my door just enough so Mother could not see me, but I was watching. Mother would not interfere, but she'd put her ear near the closed door in order to listen. After a few minutes, when she thought everything was alright, she'd leave.

When Gia and her friends tired of playing tea party, they left the room and went someplace else. I'd sneak into the parlor, sat at the little table and had my own tea party with my imaginary friends. Sometimes there were little drops of tea left over in a cup. I'd wiped them up with my finger and then lick my finger. The little drops of liquid were sweet, and smelled good. It wasn't until I was older that I found out that they were not drinking tea, but they were drinking Drambuie.

CR

Gia and I shared a bedroom. I remember that the walls were covered with wallpaper that had little pink roses with green stems that went nowhere. The flowers seemed to be floating as I listened to Mother sing her Irish songs. It was "Oh Danny Boy," "When Irish Eyes Are Smiling," and more. Every night she came to tuck us in and stayed awhile to sing to us as we drifted off.

But, early the next morning, at seven o'clock sharp, it was Father who woke us up. He'd stand on the balcony of his bedroom and sing "O Sole Mio." His voice boomed throughout the house and most likely the neighbors heard him too. I loved his singing in the mornings and Mother's tunes at night. It was a wonderful way to start and end a day. I guess that is why I wanted to become a singer.

I did not know it at the time, but our bedroom was large, I thought all girls' rooms were like mine and Gia's. There were four beds in our room: two double sized beds, one for Gia and the other for me, and two twin sized beds. The smaller beds were for the nannies. Macrina was my nanny, and her sister Conche was Gia's. Their mother was our cook her name was Dona Sofia and her son, Savoy, also worked in our home cleaning and doing odd jobs.

Above: L. to R. Gia and me in Messina.

As I grew up, I began to realize that our family was special, that we lived in a privileged world. We had two homes. Half of the year we lived in Messina. That home was big with four bedrooms, two parlors, kitchen, dinning room, baths, and servants' quarters all located on one floor. We had servants because Mother needed the help to take care of the large home.

The other part of the year we lived in Mili San Marco, a village about fifteen-miles from Messina located on the coast of the Ionian Sea. That was where our Grandfather resided in a grand old villa; he was Natale Scoglio. Born in Mandanici, Messina, Sicily, in 1857; during the era when the Spanish Bourbons ruled, however, when Grandfather was three years old, the volunteer expedition of one thousand men led by the soldier Giuseppe Garibaldi and with the support of the House of Savoy overturned the Kingdom of the Two Sicily's, and expelled King Ferdinand II. The last town to resist Garibaldi was Messina.

For the first time since the 18th century, Sicily was no longer under the yoke of the Bourbon regime. Nevertheless, the landed gentry, some of them were blood related to royalty, owned large parcels of land. Our Sicilian Grandmother, whom I never met, was Grazia Sfravara, named after Maria Pia delle Grazia, the Princess of the Two Sicily's. Grandmother was born in 1862, after the Bourbon rulers were expelled from Sicily. At that time, some of the land could be parceled off and sold. Grandmother's father was in the position to acquire the property. Upon his death, she inherited land in Mili San Marco. That was where our Grandparents met and married.

In the family villa was where their children were born, raised; and where my Grandmother died. All of her children were girls, except for one, and that was Pietro, our Father, he was born at home on October 28, 1885.

Above: L. to R. me, Grandfather Natale Scoglio, and Gia

After Grandmother passed, Grandfather, as it was with Italian families, indulged his sons, and he did a good job. Father grew up spoiled and accustomed to getting what he wanted. As a young man he fashioned himself a dandy; he wore expensive handmade suits, fine leather shoes made to order and wore white spats over the shoes. His shirts were made especially for him from fine imported silk and linen; everything in light colors, pressed and neat. When it was time for him to go to collage, he went to a first class school Columbia University, in New York. While attending school, he worked as the bookkeeper in the New York Fruit Exchange. In September 1910, he wed a girl who was born in Canada, of Irish parentage. Her name was Mary F. Tobin.

They married in the church Our Lady of Pompeii that was located at 210 Bleeker Street in Greenwich Village. It was a community church whose congregation was made up of the newly arriving immigrants from northern and southern Italy, most of whom most were living in poverty. Father Pio Parolin was the priest who performed the marriage ceremony uniting Father and Mary F. Tobin in holy matrimony.

Father Pio Parolin

Above: Father and Mary F. Tobin's marriage certificate.

The popular priest later penned a history of the church in his memoir "Father Pio Parolin, the Son of Adrian Pedo" published posthumously in 2002. He wrote that the church was poor, so much so "it was not rare that two or three of us priests would get together, longing to indulge in a glass or two of cold beer to refresh ourselves in those stifling summer days. Yet, it happened quite often that among ourselves we would not come up with the pitiable sum of ten cents! In those days, with ten cents, one could buy a bucket of beer, that is to say a quantity corresponding to ten or twelve glasses. We almost always lacked the ten cents. I recall the time I made the rather extensive rounds of going to our sacristan, Antonia Garatti, our housemaid, the lamented Magdalena, and to another priest. Finally, among the four of us we were in a position to attain the grandiose sum of ten cents with which we were able to buy ourselves that bucket of beer!"

Father Pio continued, "along with my regular religious duties, the pastor [Father Antonio Demo] assigned me the task of preparing some small theatrical productions through which funds could be raised, as small as they might be, to help reduce the huge debt. Since I knew a bit about music, I formed a small theatrical group from among the children and we often put on some musical performances where the little boys and the girls sang away. After some time, along with our little theater, we succeeded in forming a stage company among the adults of the parish. We were able to present such works as 'The Passion of Our Lord Jesus Christ' and other religious productions that enlivened the spirits ...of our dear parishioners and at the same time produced excellent financial results. In this way we attained the twofold purpose of uplifting the hearts of our poor countrymen and that of lifting the church out of the abyss into which the debts and all the consequences thereof had hurled it. The programs turned out very pleasing to our parishioners of those days; one has to remember that they had no radio, let alone television. So, there were many evenings of the week when these good people used to gather in the church basement to spend several hours in joyful peace and merriment, enjoying themselves in their simplicity as they listened to the music."

In 1927 when the church was demolished due to the construction of the 6th avenue subway extension, it was Father Pio who chronicled the history of the church that was founded by the Scalabrini fathers in October 1892,

$$\text{СЗ}$$

Father and Mary, after they wed, resided in an apartment located on Pearl Street. Father paid $60 a month rent, in 2015 dollars; the sum would be about $1,500.

Above: A view of Pearl Street, New York, 1928.

I do not know much about her except that she was a nurse. She and a medical doctor had co-authored a few articles warning 1918 New York about infectious diseases.

While Father continued to reside in New York with Mary, he would make business trips to England and Sicily. The lemon importation business was growing, and Grandfather was one of the biggest producers of the fruit in Sicily.

Grandfather cultivated extra fancy lemons that he called the "Prima Ballerina Brand." In order to get his produce to market, he had formed an export company and named it "La Limonaria."

Messina and the areas around it were and still are agricultural areas where citrus grows abundantly. At first Grandfather exported lemons, but later expanded his import business to include oranges, limes and other citrus. The export company became so successful that it exported to Europe all types of Sicilian products.

Although Sicily agriculturists were prospering, Father most likely did not want to return to provincial Mili San Marco after living in the grandness of New York City. But, after the crash of 1929, the Depression that followed, and the emergence of the dictator Benito Mussolini, Sicily began to experience economic and political turmoil.

Sicily opposed Mussolini. To gain control of Sicily, the dictator sent Cesare Mori to eradicate the Mafiosi and to restore law and order. But, his brutal tactics drove the Mafiosi underground. Mori appealed to the landed gentry, people such as Grandfather, and obliged them to support Mussolini to get rid of the Mafiosi. Two years later when Mori discovered collusion between Mussolini's Fascist government and the Mafiosi, Mussolini dismissed Mori.

Sicily paid a dear price for its opposition to Mussolini. With revenge, he turned the island into the bread basket for his armies. The once rich land was overworked and became unproductive. With that and the dictator's alignment with Adolph Hitler, Grandfather perceived the potential that Italy could be thrust into another war.

From 1910 until 1932, Father made business trips from New York to Liverpool. To cross the Atlantic transportation was by ship. Shipping was an important factor for La Limonaria's success. Grandfather sent his Ballerina lemons to Europe and to the United States by boat. As time passed Father became friendly with the sea captains of several vessels and knew the seaports, especially Liverpool, which was a busy and a wild international port that attracted an assortment of people from many countries. There were shops that had exotic imports from far off places, and interesting businesses, one of which attracted my Father and that was photography. Well, not exactly; it was a shapely young lady that caught his attention. He had taken notice of her when she entered an photo-artist's studio. A sign above the door read: Photography Tinting, the Best in Town.

Father was a resourceful man. He discovered that she was a painter who tinted photographs and at that decided he must have a tinted photograph of himself.

In the 1930's it was fashionable and quite the thing to sit for a photograph. Afterwards, those who could afford it had their portrait tinted or colored. It was something similar to having a fine-arts portrait in oil, and almost as expensive. Father had beautiful grey colored eyes. Not from a point of egotism, but there were not many Sicilians who had eyes like his. For posterity, he thought it was necessary to record his countenance in color. After all he considered himself part of the European aristocracy.

Father took great importance in educating himself with culture, literature, art, and languages. Furthermore, he dressed as if he were the Sicilian version of the Prince of Wales. Although Father was not from an Italian aristocratic family, his refined airs of grandeur convinced many he was. While most commoners could not afford a tinted photograph, he did not consider himself common.

Pietro R. Scaglia

After the photograph was ready, he picked it up from the photographer, and then carried it to the artist's atelier where the shapely artist was employed. He made an appointment to sit for the tinting; it took three sessions to complete the process. It was he and she alone in the studio, although an intimate situation, it was quite appropriate: the artist and her subject alone. But, for him the situation was his opportunity to impress the young lady, and he did. When the tinted photograph was finished, Father returned to pick up his artwork, but this time he brought with him a gift, a courting gift. It was a pretty box that contained fragrant facial soaps that were formed in the shape of lemons from "La Limonaria."

When he presented it to Miss Eileen Sullivan, he kissed her hand. She was seventeen years old, and Father was twenty-eight years older than she. Eileen with her shock of dark auburn hair, turquoise colored eyes, pleasing figure, and Irish brogue; delightfully she caught Father's fancy.

Born in Ireland, near Scott's Hill by Tahilla; she was one of eleven children who were raised on a farm, and had come to Liverpool to find her fortune, as the Irish call it. Father was unlike the other men in Liverpool who wore work-clothes, pea jackets, and knitted caps. Father fashioned himself after the silent screen actor Rudolf Valentino's Italian chic. Sophisticated elegance, he wore handmade silk shirts; French neckties, white spats that covered his handmade Italian shoes and his cologne was seductively delicious. He spoke French, German, Italian and English. With eloquent manners, and experience in life, he knew what he wanted and how to get it.

After he met Eileen, Father never returned to the United States, or to Mary. Gia was born in Liverpool, on March 3rd, 1934. On the Civil Registry, her first name was Josephine, not Gia. She was born Josephine Grace Johanna Scoglio-O'Sullivan. They lived at 73 Canning Street, Liverpool, until Gia was a little over a year old.

When Mother became pregnant with me, Father sent a telegram to Grandfather in Mili San Marco that read: "Prepare the home, arriving with wife & baby."

Above: Gia's birth certificate

Gia was two, almost two and a half years old, when I was born. It was July sixteenth; a warm day in Mili San Marco when Mother gave birth to me at home. A point that I find curious that perhaps set Gia and I apart on very different paths in life was that our parents gave Gia English names, Josephine Grace Johanna; Johanna was our Irish Grandmother's name. On the other hand, I was given Italian names. Agata, after my Father's sister, Carmella, for my Father's sister who had died young, Maria, for the sacred Mother, Scoglio, our family name, but everyone called me Tina.

I don't remember too much before I was six, but looking at the baby pictures my mother had taken of me, I was well dressed. Mother liked to dress to the nines, and she also made sure her daughters were stylish. Even as small children, she put us in well appointed lady-like attire, and took our photograph. She enjoyed photography, a life long enthusiasm, one that I inherited. To this day, I take photos of almost everyone I meet.

From my first recollections of Gia, I wanted to be like her. I'd follow her everywhere just like a baby chick follows its mother hen. Most of the time she didn't want me around, she'd shoo me away. I cried when she rejected me, at that Mother put her arms around, and gave me a hug, then a kiss on the forehead. She turned to Gia and ever so tenderly, but with an air of importance she encouraged Gia to be more compassionate towards her baby sister. I guess Gia started to resent me. But I didn't care because Mother's suggestion allowed me to become Gia's little shadow.

Above: our mother, Eileen Sullivan

Above: Far left Mother, below Mother our nanny Conche who is holding me, Gia looking at Father smoking his pipe.

She had many friends, I don't know if it was her personality, or she was so pretty. She was taller than most of the children in the town, but, everyone seemed to be attracted to her, and wanted to be around her.

Although when I was very young, she preferred to play with her friends, but I'd tag along when I could. As I grew up, gradually she let me became part of her group of pals.

When it was time for me to go to school, I joined Gia at the Institute of Saint Anna. Even though it was a private school for the upper class children of Messina, different school levels of children shared the same classroom, what I mean was when I was in the first grade; I shared a classroom with my second grade sister.

The order of nuns who taught and administered the school was strict and self-sacrificing. Through deprivations of food and sleep, it was the sacrifice they believed made them worthy to enter into God's kingdom. But, their self sacrificing caused trauma in some children, I was one of them.

I remember the first time a sister fainted during class, where she passed out onto the floor, sprawled out unconscious in front of the children. I was stunned; I could not believe it, the impression that it made until this day I cannot forget. I turned to Gia, and saw her rolling her eyes. She had seen this drama before, and for her, this was not appropriate and unnecessary because the result of the sisters' self-sacrificing scared the younger kids. Perhaps that was the affect they strived for, I don't know, but Gia thought it was stupid. If the sisters could not take care of themselves, that was eating enough so they would not pass out during class, there had to be something wrong with their thinking.

Above: Grandfather Scoglio standing behind Gia, I am sitting on the right of them. We are at Grandfather's villa in Mili San Marco. Gia wearing a lacy cape, tied with a bow under her chin, and the bow decorated with a broach! The only thing she was missing was white gloves.

Gia recognized that I was traumatized; cleverly she changed the atmosphere for me when she smiled and said, "She'll be out for awhile, let's go to the movies." We cut class and took half of the kids in the classroom with us. Afterwards, I know it may sound mean, but I began to look forward to the next time the nun fainted.

The movie theater in Messina played a great many Italian films, but the best movies were the ones that came from America. Although Mother was Irish, and often spoke to us in English, the majority of the time at home we spoke Italian. It became my first language. I understood a great deal of English, the American movies had Italian language subtitles, but I didn't care to read them because I wanted to focus on the beautiful actresses, and actors upon the screen.

Father had arranged with the cinema's proprietor for us to have an open account. We could go as much as we wanted to the movies, but what Father didn't know was that we took almost all of our friends with us.

At the end of the month when the movie bill was presented, Father was surprised at the amount, he'd call us into his office, and said, "You girls must like to go to the movies, just look at this bill!"

"Yes, Father," Gia said. She knew as a responsible parent he had to make a comment, but he really didn't care if we spent all of his money going to the movies. Gia knew he doted on us and Mother; we could ask for the moon and he'd find someway to get it for us, even if it was a moon made of chocolate. I said nothing; I watched their "dance", as I called it, between Father and daughter. I liked to go to Father's office because when I stood in front of his desk, I looked to

43

see if there were any new additions to his collection of smoking pipes that lined its front perimeter. They were gifts from European pipe makes. The pipes were carved in different forms like that of the famous Swiss mountain the Matterhorn, common bowls shapes, and animals such as bears and tigers. The pipes were made from Briarwood, a specialty from Sicily. Father exported the wood to customers in all parts of Europe. Some of the pipe makers in appreciation for his service sent him sample pipes made from the Sicilian Briarwood.

Father would motion us to come near; we walked around the desk to one side where there was a deep desk drawer on the left of his chair. Often it would be open and inside I saw thick bundles of lira. We said thank you for the movies, kissed him on the cheek, then left.

The nuns in our school fainted regularly and with that I became accustomed to cutting class with Gia and our friends. On more than one occasion the Mother Superior summoned Gia and me into her office. I remember how tiny she was, for a person with such an important position; most likely she was a few inches less than five feet tall. She sat on a chair that looked like a throne. It was set upon a platform that was raised at least ten inches off of the floor. She told us to wait, and then she asked her secretary nun to open the anteroom door. Father walked in, he looked at us sternly, and then

Mother Superior motioned for us to go into the anteroom and to close the door. Through the door we heard Father and the grand little nun talking. We peeked through the old keyhole and saw Father taking large rolls of lira out of his jacket pockets; he counted it out and handed it to Mother Superior. She smiled, and with that we were no longer in trouble for ditching class.

Above & on the next page: Gia wearing a long white veil. Mother invented costumes for Gia and me. Then she would take our photograph. She loved photography.

Father did not reproach us because that was not his way; it was Mother who was supposed to model appropriate behavior for wealthy young Sicilian girls. Gia tried to be good, but there was something that was contradictory in her nature.

Even as a child, Gia was clever. It was the way she figured out how to buy the sweet liquors for her tea parties without Mother or Father knowing. She took me along with her when she wanted more "tea." Father had a running account at the little store where we bought our candy. The owner of the store had a son who was fond of Gia. He clerked for his father after school and that was when Gia and I bought the "candy." Gia asked for bottles of "tea," and the owner's son put them in bags for her, and then put the bill and a pencil on the counter in front of Gia. She looked at the account, erased the words Drambuie and wrote "candy." She signed it and handed it back to him.

At the end of the month, Father called us into his office and said, "You girls must really like candy because you're buying so much of it!"

We saw Father at his office, and at meal times; but he did not socialize with us. He kept his distance, or perhaps his place as the parent. He was the head of our family, and his behavior was what I call lovely stern. I remember one morning Father was angry at his butler because he had burned one of Father's beautiful handmade shirts when he was ironing it. He told him that he was fired. Mother interceded and begged Father to reconsider because it was an accident, not on purpose. For her accidents were forgivable, but for Father there was no such thing as an accident. The butler scorched the shirt because he was not paying attention, perhaps daydreaming. However, after Mother's plea, Father repealed his sentence, and the butler remained employed in our household.

Above: Gia, our Godmother Rosa Cucircotta, Gia and me.

Mother was compassionate towards those who had less. For instance after each meal the leftovers did not go into the icebox, instead, in the garden on the kitchen side of our home there were outdoor tables with benches. She fed any poor soul who was hungry. And, there were many older people who waited for whatever was leftover from our table.

Father was extremely particular about food. He would not eat anything that was not prepared fresh. For that reason, our servant, Conche, early every morning went shopping for that day's food. In Messina there were outdoor markets set up along the streets under open sided tents were local farmers brought their fresh farm goods each day. They did not keep running accounts like the business people who had brick and mortar stores; the farmers had to be paid on the spot. Mother gave Conche money to buy the food, which she did, and brought it home, and then gave the change to Mother.

I remember after awhile for some reason Father became suspect of Conche. I don't why; perhaps it was one of the other servants who informed him, but without notice, he went into Conche's quarters, pulled back the mattress on her small bed, and discovered a pile of money.

Immediately he fired her. Mother interceded with sincere pleas that Conche was not a thief. Father refused to forgive Conche, and again told her to get out. Mother reminded him that the household and the home were under her control, her realm, so to speak, and his was the family business. That he must give Mother her place in front of the servants. Ooh! Mother was a clever one, her logic was impeccable. He backed down, and she once again was the head of the household.

She spoke to Conche kindly, explaining that what she did was to embezzle. Yes, the money was given to her, but given to her in trust that she would return the portion that was not used to buy food. Mother recognized the country peasants that worked in our home had little education and often did not posses the understanding of the meaning of what they did. But, after Mother explained the situation, Conche from that day forward retuned all of the unused grocery money.

ᚼ

Nazi Invasion & Allied Response

When I was about seven years old, I remember hearing people talk about an invasion. I didn't know what it meant, but when Mother and I were in Messina, and we left our home to visit friends, or do some shopping, I began to notice an increasing presence of German soldiers in the streets. They wore dark uniforms, tall boots, carried rifles. I saw troop transport trucks moving through the streets, where the stake-bed truck bed was full of soldiers standing up, some holding on to the pickets, and in tow behind a few of the transport trucks were large guns. Jeeps and tanks joined the procession; it was like a circus parade, but not as colorful.

Mother told me quietly that we were behind the enemy lines. I did not understand what that meant, nor could I have imagined how much my life would change.

As I mentioned before, we spent half of the year in Messina and the other half in Mili San Marco, it was not unusual for us to be in Mili San Marco in July; I liked to spend my birthday there. In the middle of July 1943 we were at home when there was a big boom, and another boom; I felt the floor in of our house shake; then in the second parlor a loud crash; Gia and I ran to see what had happened. What we found was the chandelier that had hung from the ceiling now was smashed in a thousand pieces on the floor along with a bunch of rubble. In the place where it had been, I saw the blue sky. A gapping hole in the ceiling had opened up.

Father and Mother looked worried. Mother told us to gather up some clothes. She put together a few baskets of food, and some necessities, we went up to a cave in the hills of Mili San Marco. It was somewhat like a tunnel; it had an opening, and a small sort of back door hole were one could escape. Father had workmen burrow-out the cave sometime in 1942. It was our safe place to go in case violence broke out. There had been fighting between the Sicilian communists and the Mafiosi. When the communists called for massive land redistribution in Sicily, the landed gentry, our family was part of that group; in an unlikely marriage, allied themselves with the Mafiosi for protection from the communists. Moreover, when Mussolini became Prime Minister in 1922, gradually his Fascists political party took over Italy, and pushed the Mafiosi underground; Mussolini had supported Hitler's rise to power, and by early 1943 we were not hiding from the communists, but from Mussolini's Fascists and the Nazi German army.

In Messina Father was forced to close down the La Limonaria. His warehouses were broken into and raided, the contents were stolen. We were left with nothing, except Father had the land.

Looking back, it seemed as though Father had perceived the potential for war and had taken measures that would help his family to survive. Quietly he moved us to Mili San Marco, as though everything was as usual. He was aware that the Italian army was fighting the British in Libya, and Britain had been his largest source of export income. Libya was an Italian colony since 1912; however, in 1940 a fight broke out over border discrepancies with the British who ruled Egypt. It was the British Lt. General Montgomery who fought back the Italian army. But Hitler jumped into the fight because he recognized an opportunity to seize the Suez Canal. Hitler sent General Rommel and his troops into Northern Africa to aid the Italians against the British. The Americans entered the war and with the British pushed the Italians and the Nazi Germans out of Egypt, Libya and all of North Africa. Italy lost Libya, but gained 80,000 Germans Nazis. When the Germans entered Sicily, Mussolini was cautious; he had said that once the Germans come in to Sicily, we will never be able to get them out.

Sicily found itself caught up in a new war. There were German soldiers all over the island. Their key stronghold was Randazzo, and they held other strong positions along the eastern seacoast.

In January 1943, General Eisenhower had said that after Africa had been finally cleared of the enemy, the island of Sicily should be assaulted and captured as a base for operations against Southern Europe, to open the Mediterranean to the shipping of the United Nations. He called for a meeting of the top allied Generals, he wanted them to form a plan of attack on Sicily; the maneuver became known as Operation Husky.

The Germans penetrated into the mountainous areas of the interior of Sicily. Their lines of advance would be restricted to a few existing roads and due to their skill of mining and demolition the enemy's progress would be slow. They booby trapped Messina Strait with mines and had set up coast defense batteries.

Messina at the north - eastern tip of the island was regarded as the most important object because this strategically situated port, as might be expected, could furnish initially the means of entry of Axis reinforcements from the mainland.

Because of Messina's location, Father had perceived that there could be fighting in between the Axis and the Allieds.

Above: Gia left & me right, in Mili San Marco, we are on the balcony of the parlor where a few years later in 1943 the ceiling crashed down from the vibration of the exploding Allied bombs.

As he planned we were safe in the cave, I remember that night, the first night we were there, Mother lit a candle that had a pungent order, and the light it gave off was dim. I heard water dripping somewhere in the cave. Outside there was boom, boom... bombs exploding, I felt the vibrations from the explosions, then guns from the ground shooting, loud and big bang, bang, bang. We were scared not only from the sounds, but what they intended: death. Mother huddled us together. I was shaking, and trembling, but Gia was quite, and kept still. Throughout the night the bombs went on exploding, it was amazing that although the bombs were hitting the ground around Messina that was about 15 miles away, the sounds waves traveled through the air and with that the vibrations.

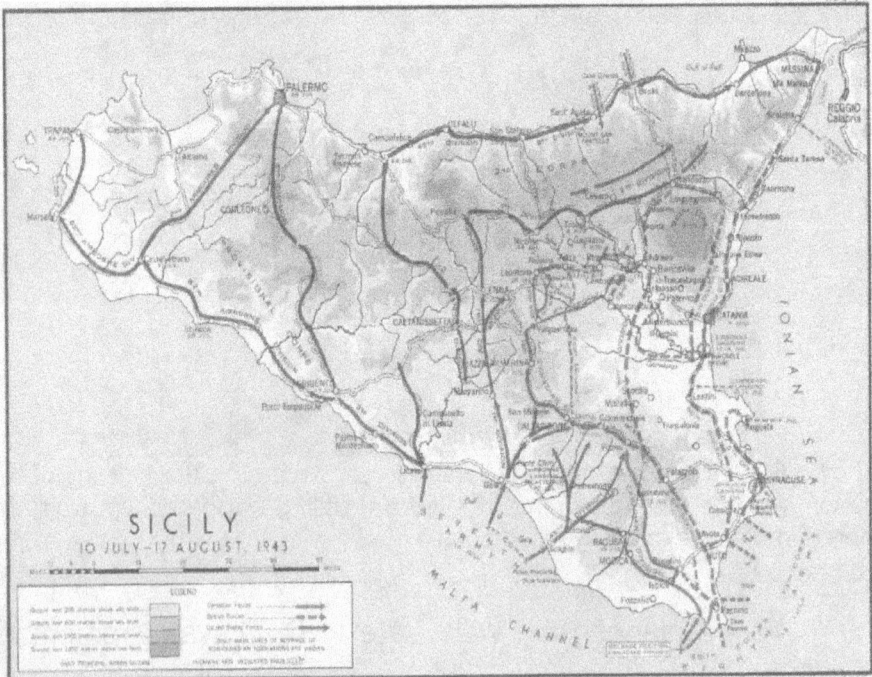

SICILY
10 JULY–17 AUGUST, 1943

Later I found out that during the time the Allied forces attacked the Nazi German and Italian Armies in Sicily there had been forty-two thousand air attacks on Messina and the surrounding areas, some 350 tons of bombs fell on that region. But, the first night we were in the cave, the air strikes seemed to never end. It was impossible to sleep because with each explosion I felt insecure, that my little life was in danger. The cave was high enough on the hill so that we could see some of the splashes of light over the Messina Strait. "What's that?" I asked Mother.

"It is the Allied forces taking Messina," she said.

At the time, I did not know what an Allied was or what she meant, but Mother fearful of the Nazi German soldiers and the Allied bombs made us stay in the cave. When we ran out of food, Mother taught us how to scavenger. Well, it was not exactly what I called food, we looked for herbs, roots, and what ever that she showed us was not poisonous. One herb in particular, I remember, that she insisted we eat was "porcelina" as it was known in Italian.

Purslane is the English name. It is a short plant with green oval shaped leaves; some people consider it a weed because it grows abundantly. But that plant has Omega 3 fatty acids more than any leafy vegetable; ten to twenty times more melatonin and antioxidants than any other vegetable. It has many vitamins, also iron, magnesium, zinc, and potassium.

People in Southern Europe eat the plant, but it is not used much in the United States.

Purslane grew wild on the hills in Mili San Marco, and we ate it raw. Later on I discovered that the people who ate Purslane during the war when food was in short supply survived much better than those who did not eat it.

It was a long while that we lived in the cave. On the dirt floor we tried to sleep at night, but the noise of the bombs and the shootings broke up our rest. We became sleep deprived added to that during the day there was the misery of scrounging or foraging for something to eat. One day Mother had had enough of eating boiled foraged food. Most likely exhausted from the lack of food, sleep, and stressed out from fear, perhaps she was not thinking clearly, but she took me by the hand and said, "Come on." Gia did not want us to leave, but Mother told her to stay in the cave until we returned.

She led me towards town. When we reached the main street, I remember seeing German soldiers with rifles and guns on each side of the road. There were also tanks and all sorts of military things. Mother did not walk on the sidewalk, fearful, I suppose, of getting too close to the men, where a soldier could touch us or worse steal one of us or both of us! Instead, we walked down the middle of the road. I remember seeing the soldiers. That scene was unforgettable: it was me and Mother surrounded with hundreds of Nazi German soldiers with guns and rifles. When I think about it now, I suppose Mother did not take Gia with us because she was tall, pretty, & looked more womanly than me, Gia would have drawn too much attention. While I was very much a little girl, perhaps Mother's actions sent a subliminal message to the soldiers that she was not a spy or a prostitute; but she was a mother taking care of her child. The Germans did not stop us.

When we got back to the cave with the food, Mother told us that she did not expect to see so many soldiers. Terrified at the situation, she feared being stopped and then questioned. Although she spoke very good Italian, she had an accent. Easily recognizable in conversation that she was a foreigner. If she had turned back the Germans might have stopped us, and if we continued forward we could have been stopped. She had to go on with purpose. It was lucky for us that we were not discovered because we could have been arrested and taken to a concentration camp like what happened to her good friend Mrs. Tarentino.

An Irish immigrant like Mother, Mrs. Tarentino had married one of the riches men in Messina. Her home was grand and she needed many servants to manage it. Before the war, her servants did the grocery shopping. But when the Nazi Germans invaded, the servants were in-scripted, arrested, or they ran away. Mrs. Tarentino was forced to do her own marketing. One day she needed to buy meat and went to the town butcher. He like some of the business owners had become a fascist, either to survive, or because he believed in the political cause. When Mrs. Tarentino asked for the meat, the butcher laughed in her face and said, "So now that you don't have any servants, you have to come in person for your meat." At that she slapped him across the mouth. He called the Gestapo. She was arrested and afterwards spent a year in a concentration camp.

Father was with us most of the time in the cave, but when he left, I remember once he brought back a big pot of potatoes. They were dirty, scrawny, potatoes that looked like he had taken them out of someone's garbage. But, it didn't make any difference what they looked like, we ate them.

On another occasion, he brought back a little crystal set that operated on a battery. Father spoke and understood the German language. The Nazis had set up a temporary radio station in Sicily. Father listened to the reporter, his name was Lutz Koch, and then translated what was said to us in Italian. The broadcast was about the Nazis side of the war: "our soldiers are tortured by the lack of water," the reporter said. "Day and night Allied artillery drive bombers screech low over our heads. If we are near the coast, heavy Allied navel guns enter into this dance of death."

"After British paratroops suddenly descend into this pandemonium and attack us from the rear, right from the beginning we could not compete with the Allied field batteries and tanks."

On another occasion, Father told us a story that he said was spreading like wildfire throughout the American and British armies on Sicily; it was about a British provost marshal capturing an Italian general and his aide-de-camp after a thrilling 45 minute chase up and down the slopes of Mount Edna. All three mounted on donkeys.

It seemed that the provost marshal received word of two suspicious characters in civilian clothes had been sighted riding donkeys along the lower path of the mountain not far from the newly captured British position. The provost marshal went out to investigate, found them and attempted to approach them on foot. The two men urged their donkeys up the steep, sloping road.

So the Britisher found himself a donkey and followed.

Not far away, he saw the two Italians again and when they saw him, they rode farther along the road.

The provost marshal slapped his donkey on the rump, kicked the little beast in the ribs, and crying "Tallyho!" charged off in full pursuit.

Up and down the steep mountain roads, through pine tree groves, and across little streams of water the chase went on; the Britisher gradually gaining.

After 45 minutes of hard riding he caught and collared the two Italians, forcing them to dismount. One of them immediately declared that he was General Fiumara, the second in command of the proud Italian Napoli Division. To prove it, from the donkey's saddle bags he pulled out a magnificent gold braided general's uniform. The other man meanwhile produced a uniform almost as fancy and announced that he was the general's aide-de-camp.

As prisoners of war, the Italians insisted on changing back into their uniforms then and there; then allowed themselves to be taken back to the British lines.

The provost marshal sighed, "All I needed was what you Yanks call a lasso."

Officially it was announced that General Fiumara had been captured "with donkey."

We enjoyed Father's "intelligent" reports, although his entertainment lightened the mood, it seemed that it was forever that we lived in the cave. Although I was eight years old when I started living in the cave and nine when I left, I will never forget the smells inside of the cave, the tastes of the roots and the herbs we ate, but most of all I remember how scared I was.

Gia changed during that time, perhaps it was puberty, becoming a young woman, or maybe it was the terror of war and the constant threat of death. Pensively she sat at night in the candle light, quietly alone in her thoughts.

Close to the end of the bombing and gunfire, we found out that the British Commando Unit 2, an equivalent to the U.S Navy Seals, had landed at Scaletta, which was about seven miles from where we were. They had entered far behind the German lines. Upon arriving they met with a great deal of hand to hand combat. Four Brits perished in the battle, but the Commando Unit successfully pushed back the Germans. Afterwards they headed on the road that passed Mili Marina, towards Messina; their mission was to deactivate the German mines in the Messina Strait. That Unit arrived in Messina before General Patton.

One night, after about eleven months living in the cave; a Nazi German soldier invaded. When I saw him, I froze, I wanted to cry, but I didn't. I could see in Mother's eyes at that moment she didn't know what to do. On the other hand, Gia was calm, had no expression on her face. For her it was inevitable situation, why were we hiding? The Germans were everywhere; for them we were no more than collateral damage.

When he brandished his rifle at us; pointed it in a threatening way, grunting something in German, I felt a knot growing in my stomach, and my throat muscles tighten. Gia was quite. Mother put her arms around us and we backed away from the soldier. She pushed as far as she could from him. Gia's face was flat, no emotions. During the time he was in our cave, he did not sleep; he kept crouched near the cave opening, continually scanning the area outside.

After awhile, Mother regained her composure; most likely she thought to herself that if the Nazi had not killed us by now, that he would not, that was unless we gave him a reason. Perhaps he had a family, children and a wife, he was compassionate, and on the other hand, what if he was looking for his friends, other Nazi soldiers?

Instead of cowering like a little mouse waiting for who knows what, her Irish rose up and she was determined to do something to protect her children. But, the question was what could a thirty-one year old woman who was five foot four inches tall, and barely weighted one hundred and twenty pounds do against a big Nazi German soldier with a rifle?

Later she told us that she remembered a stanza from a Walt Whitman poem, it said:

> Disguise our bondage,
> as we will;
> But it is a woman,
> who rules us still.

That was it! Of course, kindness and cordiality were a woman's defense weapons. With a smile and a kind heart, she offered him food, a cup of our boiled forage; that was all we had. When she handed him the cup, he grabbed it from her, but didn't eat until he saw her eat from her cup. With an emotionless face, he said, "Danka,"

At early morning's light, he exited the cave, escaping somewhere into the rugged mountains. After he left, Mother and I cried, but Gia didn't, I heard her say, "Danka."

Mother thought the German soldier might have been a deserter. Attempting to escape both the German and the Allied forces; he needed a place to hide, how grateful she was that he didn't hurt us, but if the Germans were running away, there could be more soldiers looking for a place to hide. Fortunately, there were no more intruders. We stayed in the cave until Father came.

After the Allied forces took over Sicily, we returned to Messina. "La Limonaria" was closed down, the warehouses looted, we hardly had anything to eat, Father needed to find work. He discovered that the Allied forces were looking for translators. When he interviewed with General Omar Bradley, he was hired immediately. Soon we had money to buy food.

When I look back at that time I lived in the cave, I wonder why that experience had been in our life's path. Why did we have to experience the heavy thumb of the Nazis and then the Americans? Why did we have to feel the continual possibility of our demise, the fear, and the deprivations, I have asked myself many times: what was our Karmic lesson from this?

Although Gia and I were together during the war, we survived it differently; on the one hand, I was scared of the bombs, living in the cave was terrible, insecure of not having enough food, and the Nazis soldiers frightened me, but I felt the security of having Mother and my big sister who I believed protected me and would make sure everything would be alright. On the other hand, Gia was older and her perceptions were different. Of course she knew Mother would fight like an alley cat to protect her children, but if something happened to her, then what? There was a great possibility that our family could have been wiped out. If the Nazis discovered that Father was pro-Allied, as punishment, they could have imprisoned him and us, and or he could have been shot. But we could also have been killed by the Allied forces. Towards the end of the fighting, Allied light and medium fighter bombers repeatedly crisscrossed the north-eastern part of Sicily with explosives. Kitty-hawks and War-hawks joined the attack on sea-craft in the Messina Strait. There were so many explosions I felt my teeth rattle.

They bombed Messina with such violence that afterwards, some said the devastation was similar to that of the great Messina earthquake that occurred in January of 1909. At that time the city was flattened and eighty-thousand people died.

For Gia, living with the continual fear of disaster and death during a time in her life when she was entering young womanhood, I now understand the emotional trauma she experienced. I watched her becoming quite, pensive, and emotionless, she withdrew during stressful times. There was no drama, no show of emotions; she seemed to accept the possibility of her death.

But later in life, she often stepped over the line of accepting death into daring death. Strange behaviors for a rich girl who came from a respectable, wealthy, Catholic family, but it was the war that left Gia scared and damaged emotionally.

During that time, when soldiers came under fire from modern warfare, overly stressed and exhausted, they could become mentally confused. That circumstance was called shell-shocked. Modernly, however, the condition became Post Traumatic Distress Syndrome. In 1945, there was no therapy for Gia; instead, she had to find a way to deal. Looking back on her life after the war, I understand why as an adult when faced with stressful situations she reacted oddly, unfortunately sometimes dangerously.

Father, like Gia, most likely was also war traumatized. During those years he endured the Fascist threats and Nazis taking over; he was put into a difficult position between that group and the Allied forces to which he was loyal.

During World War I, he lived and worked in New York; and as an American patriot, he signed up and carried a Draft Card. Although he was not called for service because he was married, he was ready to go if the draft opened up to married men. Father loved America, and after the Sicily invasion, he worked for the Allied Control Commission.

Our next door neighbor in Messina who was a very popular medical doctor joined the fascists. At the time, I did not understand why, but almost every weekend we were invited into his home with his wife and family for a party. A great many of his friends and their families also attended. I remember there was wonderful food, and live music. I danced, well, not exactly, I'd put my feet on top of a neighbor's or friend's shoes, when he moved, I hung on. Whoosh... I went around the dance floor, it was fun. Then there was singing, we sang Italian songs, and we ate sweets like pies and cookies. It was our, meaning Mother, Gia, and me, big social event. When it was time for us to go home, often Father came for us, but never would he take a step inside the doctor's home. However, as the fascist population increased in Messina, our doctor - neighbor began to wear an Italian army uniform thus outwardly showing his allegiance. Father kept a cordial distance from him and all of the local fascists.

☙

The following letter is the only copy I have. Because it is difficult to read, I've transcribed it below:

Allied Control Commission
Province of Messina
Messina, 8 August, 1944
Subject: Pietro Scoglio

To Whom It May Concern:
This is to certify that Pietro Scoglio was employed by the Allied Military Government from August 1943 until August 1944, as Interpreter and Translator of the English and Italian languages.
Throughout his period of service Mr. Scoglio gave entire satisfaction by the able and intelligent performance of

his duties and the standard of his work was always of the highest.

Signed: C. Norman Ramsey, Lt-Colonel, Finance, Provincial Commissioner, Messina

Above: The letter my Father received for his work during the war.

&

Reconnecting

After the Allies chased the Axis out of Messina, everyone in Sicily celebrated. There were people in the streets singing and dancing, parties going on everywhere. We returned to Messina, to our home. I appreciated how good it was to sleep in my bed, to have food to eat, and have a bathroom.

Father was rebuilding the business, and re-connecting with clients. He often entertained at home, inviting people, those that he had known and had done business with from all parts of Europe.

I remember on more than one occasion, when General Montgomery was in Messina, he visited Father in our home. I was ten years old when I peeked through the keyhole in the living room door and watched Father and the General talking and smoking pipes. They were in our smaller parlor that had two medium sized davenports upholstered in red velvet, and the chairs were positioned on an angle like the letter "Vee." It was a comfortable arrangement where one could talk to the person sitting on the other sofa, yet was not forced to directly look at the other person, but instead gaze at the fire in the fireplace. From my view point through the keyhole, I saw the back of Father's head and the General's profile. When the General returned to England, he corresponded with Father. It was exciting when Father read the letters to us.

Because of Father's relationship with the Allied forces, he was in a position where he helped many Messina business friends to rebuild and to reopen their stores. Building supplies were at a big demand, yet short in supply, along with store merchandise, but Father also knew Captains of cargo ships. When permissions were needed, Father knew who to ask. He had earned the trust of not only the occupying Allied military, but of the town's business people as well. They were grateful to him and admired him.

After we returned to Messina, gradually our lives normalize. Gia, who had been interested in theater before the war, decided that she would put on theatrical shows in our home and charge five cents per admission. Because the local theaters were closed, or had been destroyed from the bombing, Gia thought she had a captive market. She starred and I was the co-star.

In our biggest living room, about four feet from the back wall, she placed two large folding screens on each side of a platform that she had made to use as our stage. Behind the screens was where we kept and changed our costumes. I remember that she designed outfits for us that were rather skimpy for the era. They were two piece swimsuits, but more like bikinis. Then she tied long flowing scarves around our waists and we held scarves in our hands. We'd dance, and spin around. The scarves flowed around us gracefully. She'd lift me up; swing me around, all very terpsichorean. Many of the town's people attended our few performances; they were kind and applauded our efforts.

Father and Gia frequently had guests in our Messina home. Gia was popular and had so many friends whom she entertained with tea parties, with card games, or with an occasional theatrical event. Father, on the other hand, invited his friends and business associated for lunch and sometimes dinners. Father believed in the old adage: They treat you like they see you. For that reason he liked to have his home beautifully kept, there was good food to eat, Father dressed impeccably, and he liked to have his daughters looking well-dressed all of the time.

Father asked the tailor come to our house; he arrived with bolts of fabric and books that had pictures of dresses. We decided which dresses we liked and then choose the fabric. The tailor took our measurement and made each of us a new wardrobe. Even our shoes were hand made especially for us.

Mother took photos of us in our new garments. From the outside, Gia looked wonderful, she had a beautiful face, her body was tall, thin and shapely, but I could tell that something had changed within her. She was quieter and more withdrawn than before the war.

Left to Right: Me, Father, & Gia; we are modeling our new dresses.

ଓଓ

Ireland

One afternoon, Captain Kelly, Father's good friend, was having lunch with us at our home in Messina. He was a well-received and a frequent visitor. At the dining room table, during the meal, he'd entertain us with stories of his life at sea. Gia and I enjoyed his visits because he was a pleasant man, wore a smile, and often brought along his First Mate who was young, and cute!

While Gia had had friends who were males, after the war, she began to reconsider the term "friend." When we were in Mili San Marco, a young man, Frederico Silvestro, used to invite Gia and me on walks. I remember one time Frederico, myself and some other friends; we were at the pier in Mili Marina, sitting on the edge of the wharf, watching the sunset, talking and laughing. When it became dark, I said, "Let's go home."

But, Gia said, "Wait." At that she dived off the edge of the pier. I looked at the others; I was astonished that she would jump into the dark water on a starless night. We couldn't see anything we only heard the splash of water.

I began to get worried, and looked over the edge of the pier but I couldn't see her. Then from the dark Gia climbed out of the water, stood up and in her hand she held something that was wiggling, when I got a little closer, what she was holding up was a big eel! It was flip-flopping around madly, and she was laughing, but I didn't think it was funny. "Ok, I'm ready to go home," she said and threw the eel back into the sea.

I don't know why she did that; maybe she was trying to impress Frederico that she was fearless. However, afterwards, I don't remember seeing him again.

Above: Gia and me in our cabana at Lido Beach.

At the dinning table, Gia watched the Captain's First Mate. Tall, good looking, and well mannered, he was especially polite towards our servant Conche who served the meal. When she brought him the tray of meat, he picked up the serving fork from the tray, and with it stabbed a piece of the meat lifted it from the tray, and placed it onto his plate, when he returned the fork to the serving tray, he looked up into Conche's eyes, smiled and said, "Thank you."

Gia observed Conche: she smiled with her lips when she replied, "You're welcome." But she also smiled with her eyes. Gia got it! Conche was flirting.

She was about ten years older than Gia, and had been her nanny when Gia was a toddler. Working as a servant, perhaps, for Conche was not what she planned for her future.

Father was talking to the Captain, when suddenly he turned to us and asked,

"Would you like to meet your Irish grandmother?

Without the slightest hesitation, "Yes!" we said.

The next morning on the dock in Messina we watched Captain Kelly's ship *The Heron* being loaded up. Although it was a cargo ship, there were a few cabins for passengers.

The first day at sea it was fun to be on onboard a ship. We got to know the small number of passengers. The First Mate was cordial and joined in socializing and playing games with us in the passenger lounge. The voyage was fun and wonderful until we came to the Straights of Gibraltar.

Above: Aboard *The Heron*, L to R: Gia, with her binoculars, Captain Kelly, Me, Mother, & another passenger.

I awoke in the morning being flung about in my bed. I looked out of the cabin porthole and saw giant waves exploding against the towering yellow colored cliffs of Gibraltar. A storm was raging outside. The boat creaked from the violent waves crashing down, and then the ship jumped upward, only to be brought downward again as it rocked from side to side while stabilizing its equilibrium. *The Heron* seemed small and insignificant against the powerful ocean. I thought for sure that we were going to crash against the jagged edges of the cliffs. When Gia saw that I was distressed and fearful, she put her arms around me, hugged me and encouraged me to lie down, to be calm, "it will be over soon," she said. Kindly and compassionate towards her scared little sister, she was wonderful that day. The three of us, Mother, Gia, and me, became sea sick during the squall, but somehow, I know it seems odd, but the experience brought us closer.

Although the storm horrified me, and Mother was worried, Gia on the other hand was unmoved. Inwardly cool, outwardly pensive, it reminded me how she was when we lived in the cave, with the bombs, and the gunfire exploding everywhere, she merely stared as if she was looking past life into eternity.

I remember on our voyage, she spent a good deal of time by herself with her binoculars, seldom she was without them. For hours she'd be looking through them, at far off things, contemplative and alone.

The Heron docked at Liverpool to windy, cold, and gloomy weather. It was such a contrast to sunny Sicily. From Liverpool we rode a bus to London. We shopped for new clothes, for the latest English fashions. When Mother was satisfied that we looked stylish, we left for Ireland.

By boat we went from Liverpool, England to Cork, Ireland. Mother hired a car; our driver took us to Tahilla by way of the Ring of Kerry. The road stretched far into the country. For miles we saw nothing but wide open spaces. He stopped on the thoroughfare where a pathway crossed. We looked down the little lane and saw a house made of stone. We were at Scott's Hill by Tahilla- Mother's family property. It looked like a farm, maybe one could call it a ranch, I saw barnyard animals, and horses. We walked to the house; the family had seen us approach and came outside to greet us. It was the first time I met Uncle Denie, and Aunt Lizzy. They hugged us and kissed us; Denie called me and Gia pretty lasses.

I walked into the home and for the first time saw our Irish Grandmother Johanna Shagrue-Sullivan. She was remarkable; I had never seen a woman eighty-nine years old who seemed as if she were forty. She was slender with a beautiful posture. Although her face showed a long life, her body, however, was strong and active, especially after having give birth to eleven children and raised them as well. She was in the kitchen making Irish soda bread over an open fire!

The first morning we were up early and right away went to the barn to collect eggs. We took the eggs back up to the house for Mother. We had never done this type of thing in Sicily. When we saw her in the kitchen preparing food with our Irish Grandmother, it was odd to see her cooking in a home without servants.

Above: Gia, Mother and me, our Mother was always ever so stylish.

Everyday Gia rode horses. Daringly, she'd grab the horse's mane, swing her body over and straddle her legs on its back; she rode without a saddle. I'd watch her gallop around the countryside, the faster she rode the more she enjoyed it. Fearlessly she maneuvered the animal to jump every obstacle in her way. She was not a dainty or frilly girl; she was a tomboy in many aspects, more like a son to our Father. It was as if she wanted to live up to Father's family image and carry on the Scoglio family tradition of bravery, and pride. She'd be gone for hours, riding adventurously everywhere. She was in control of the steed and most likely for that reason had no fear at all.

Our first days there flew by quickly, and just as fast we accustomed ourselves to the Irish lifestyle. It was so unlike what we knew in Messina, with the Sicilian formalities before and after the war. In Ireland there was no house staff to do the shopping, cooking, cleaning and serving. We set the dinner table, and served the food. Afterwards, we cleaned up.

I discovered that the Irish don't like to be the servants of others; they serve no master and are fiercely independent. They put such a great value on freedom. An incident occurred while we were there showed me the extreme attitude change from what I had known in Italy. While we were staying at Grandmother's farm, a high society woman from New York City came to visit. The woman was a friend of our Aunt Kate who had moved to New York, and worked as a nurse. The friend arrived to dinner in a chauffeur-driven limousine and had her driver wait in the car. As a large and lovely meal was being put on the table, Uncle Denie discovered that the poor man was out in the car. My Uncle could not tolerate the notion of someone outside his door uninvited to his dinner table. My Aunt's New York friend was shocked when Uncle Denie asked us to set another place at the table and then invited the chauffeur to eat with them.

My Irish family was noble. They, like most Irish people, would not permit the ways of the outside world to be forced upon them, especially if contrary to what they feel inside. The Irish are not accustomed to becoming conditioned, brainwashed and desensitized by outside influences. I remember when a group of wealthy Americans chose Ireland as a place to build high-rise apartments, they explained that it would be for more people to enjoy the uniquely tranquil environment; the Irish government rejected their proposal. They weren't about to give up their lands to foreigners who wanted to profit from the natural beauty of the land of Ireland.

The land is so much a part of their freedom and so is their freedom of speech, especially when it comes to telling a good tale.

"Ah, 'tis a story you want?" our uncle asked us. "Then let me tell you about the monster that lives in the lake."

Uncle Denie got Gia wound up with that one. He was talking about the lake nearest the farm. He continued, "Our beast 'tis not as big as Nessy of Lock Ness and that being so because our lake's a wee bit smaller," he said. Then added,

"The monster comes out on starless nights, when the sky is as dark as the inside of Saint Patrick's tomb."

I suppose Uncle Denie thought that his well raised nieces would not be traipsing around the countryside in the dark to see a monster, but he underestimated Gia. Adamantly she wanted to see the monster, and likewise I was curious.

At the end of every day, as the sun was setting, we'd start off towards the lake. Along the way, there were many fresh-water springs that fed the lake. They bubbled up out of the earth and the rocks. Gia and I enjoyed finding the little springs where we could taste the fresh water. We'd reach the lake by nightfall. On one evening, we were at the lake ... it was located miles from anything. The night had grown especially murky. Gia thought it was dark enough that the monster would come out of the lake. Wanting to get closer to the lake to get a better look at the surface of the water, she being daring and inquisitive went to the water's edge. I stayed behind. Then I heard Gia screaming "Tina, Tina!"

"Oh, it's the monster; he's got her!" I thought. Her screams become desperate. I ran to where she was and found her stuck in quicksand. As she was fighting to get out, the quicksand pulled her further down. I was afraid of falling in myself. I groped in the darkness until I found a fallen tree bough, and held it out to her. I put myself on solid ground;

she grabbed the branch and pulled herself out of the quicksand. We were both terrified. We ran back to the house. This was the first time that I saved my sister's life, but it would not be the last.

Except for the incidence at the lake and Gia riding the horse all over the countryside, it was idle time at Scott's Hill. The atmosphere was relaxed, but Mother wanted a change. Accustomed to Italian social life, she decided we should go to Kenmare and rent a house. At Scott's Hill we were miles away from neighbors and Mother was a social person. Also, she wanted to get us back into school because we were in school when we left Sicily. Kenmare had a convent school and we could rent a house nearby. It was fine with Gia and me because there would be children there for us to make friends with.

Our Irish Mother Superior was Sister Patrick. She was far more lenient than the sisters at Saint Anna Institute. We liked Sister Patrick because she was warm, friendly and informal.

The most difficult thing for us to adjust to in school was learning the language. Irish was what they called it, but it was also known as Gaelic. However, the Scottish people as well call their language Gaelic. I learned that there was Irish-Gaelic and Scottish-Gaelic.

At school the Irish was a requirement. But I found it so difficult that I did a good deal of faking. I remember miming the Irish songs we sang in the choir. The words were tongue-twisters; it was not surprising that the language hasn't become more international. The Irish people liked to drop in a spattering of their language while speaking English; they use it as if admiring treasured family heirlooms. An Irish-Gaelic word or expression here and there makes one less homesick of olden times. When we returned to Italy, the language lessons were something I did not miss.

The priest there at the convent school was different. Not as serious as those in Sicily, he'd smile, and often gave us a little money out of his pocket after school so we could go to the store and buy candy.

On the subject of sweet treats, I remember there was a young single woman who ran the candy store in Kenmare. She was attractive, except for a slightly dark line of hair that grew above her upper lip. It was the mustache that my sister thought distracted from her beauty. She wanted to help the young maiden to improve her looks, so she offered to cut off the facial hair. They went into the back room of the store and with a razor Gia shaved off the hair. The girl was grateful and they became friends.

Often after school, Gia would go to the store where her new friend worked and played store-keeper; she's give out free candy to her friends. But when I came in, she made me pay for my candy!

My sister thought that our parents spoiled me. In her mind, she attempted to rectify their mistake by doing the opposite, to be stern and strict with me. Such was the case with the candy. With this attitude towards me, she kept me from joining in some fun activities.

Being far away from Father and in Kenmare away from other family members, Gia began to challenge Mother's position of authority. An example was one evening when Mother went to a party with some of her friends. The couple had two children in their early teens that stayed with us while the adults went out. Before they left, Gia and the two teenagers snuck some beers and hid them in the closet. After the parents were gone, I watched them take the beers out of the closet and drink them all. By the time the adults returned, Gia and the others were drunk. When Mother asked me what was wrong, I didn't know what to say. The next day, Mother reprimanded Gia. This kind of rebel activity was beginning to occur frequently.

Gia and her friends often got a hold of Ireland's cheapest cigarettes. They were called Wood Fine and cost five pennies a pack. One day I saw Gia and her friends hiding in the woods smoking. Gia called me over, had me sit down and to try a puff. I began to cough and became very sick, I vomited and vomited. Meanwhile, Gia laughed, but I never smoked again.

While Mother was gentle and nice through most of her older daughter's mischievousness, Gia was becoming increasingly rebellious. When Mother scolded her, it had no effect. Gia was at that age when she wanted to do what she wanted to do and to hell with everyone else.

Above: On our confirmation day.

Uncle Denie and Aunt Lizzy, who were Gia's godparents, felt it was time for her and me to be confirmed in the church. While we were in Ireland, we attended catechism, and prepared for the ceremony.   Meanwhile Mother ordered beautiful gowns for each of us, they were meant to be cherished keepsakes. I remember on my sister's confirmation day she looked like an angel. A reception followed the ceremony, but Gia disappeared from the party with a girlfriend. Mother was angry that she left; however, a couple of hours later when she came back, our Mother could not believe her eyes. The keepsake dress Gia wore was grease-stained and torn. She had gone bicycling.

One day, Gia and I returned home after school, after our Irish Jig lessons, we found Mother was bed laden. We had never seen her like that before and we were shocked. Mother had a blood-soaked bandage across her forehead. When we saw this we rushed to her bedside. She began scolding us with a shallow and weak voice. Although she was talking to both of us, what she was saying was directed to Gia. She said that she brought us on a nice vacation to Ireland and that we wouldn't do anything that she asked us to do. That it made her ill; feebly she continued that she could not control us without Father. She kept this up until we were crying, frightened and apologetic. Then she burst into laughter.

Mother had contrived the whole situation. She had gone as far as putting ketchup on the bandage. Mother had given us our first lesson in acting.

After we were in Kenmare for awhile, Mother thought it would be a good idea that we purchase a summer home there; in order that we would have our own place to stay in when we returned.

Through the help of a real estate agency, she found a charming cottage on the outskirts of Kenmare. It looked like a home perfect for Hansel and Gretel; located beside a bubbling brook; inside there was a giant stone fireplace and the windows were lattice crisscrossed leaded hand blown glass. Gia and I loved it and pleaded with her to buy it. She started the purchase, but prior to the final closing, she received a letter from Messina.

Before we left Sicily, Mother had asked the maid who worked next door to keep an eye on the servants in our home; to report if there was any problems. The letter Mother received read that Father had fired all of the servants in our home, and replaced them with three beautiful young and sexy women.

At that Mother decided it was time to return home. Gia and I were not pleased about leaving because we had a wonderful new group of friends, some with red hair and freckles.

Our relatives were sorry to see us go; they loved having us there and made us promise to return to Ireland. Gia and I kept our promise.

When Gia returned to Ireland in 1970, it was a quiet time for her. A wonderful visit, she spent most of her time sketching the likeness of the Irish countryside on sheets of paper, and drawing portraits of Uncle Denie and Aunt Lizzy. Her life at Scott's Hill was different to her life in Hollywood. The most socializing she participated in was an evening drink. Denie and Lizzy had sold a piece of their land to a British company that had built a country resort on it. Denie and Lizzy went to bed early in the evening so that Gia could go to the nightspot and watch the activities.

On my return to Ireland as an adult, I became very much a part of country while I was there. I was sad that I could not stay longer; it reminded me of Mother's hasty departure so many years past.

೮೩

When we left Ireland with Mother, she did not send word to Father that we would arrive in Messina. She planned to show up unexpectedly just to find out what was going on.

At our home in Messina, Mother walked in the front door and saw the young sexy women sitting in our living room talking, laughing, and eating snacks. "Oh," she said, "I understand that you are the new employees. Well, your break time is over. Get up and go to work!"

She had them scrubbing the floors, cleaning the walls, working as they should. Their employment didn't last long. Afterwards, Mother hired back the former servants.

൙

Our Return to Messina

It was good to be home once more. I noticed the way Father treated us that he recognized we had changed. Perhaps more mature; maybe one could say a wee bit more sophisticated because we had traveled by sea to a foreign country, lived in Ireland, became familiar with a new language Gaelic, and confirmed in the Church. I suppose for Father we were no longer his little girls; he must have figured that soon we would begin to take our proper place in the world.

Mother was pleased to be again in our home with Father. Although she was suspicious of his motivations of getting rid of our faithful and long time servants, she never reproached him about it or about the young sexy replacements, who were useless and lazy. I do not remember one incident that Mother and Father had a disagreement. She was sweet and loving, he was caring, but in a manly fashion which for him meant taking care that his family did not go without. However, personally, I suspect that when we were in

Ireland, Father missed us very much. And he knew that Mother was clever, perhaps had a spy in the neighborhood with whom she corresponded. He wanted us to return to Messina, but he would never say it, or ask Mother to return. Instead, I think he created a situation that he knew would bring Mother back immediately.

When Mother rehired our former servants, everyone returned except for Conche. She did not come back. What happened? Did she find another place of employment? When I asked about her, Father told us while we were away Captain Kelly and his young First Mate when they were in port often dined with him. After awhile Father recognized that the First Mate and Conche seemed to have a special appeal for one another. Although Conche was not his daughter or a family relative, Father was the head of our home, and to give Father his place, the First Mate asked permission to see Conche socially. Father said yes, and a month later they were married in the Church. When she became Mrs. First Mate, she sailed away on *The Heron* with her new husband for the American port of New York. Upon their arrival, the First Mate left the sea and opened a business on dry land.

Gia said that she knew it; there was something special about the way Conche and the First Mate looked at each other.

We were happy that Conche and the First Mate found each other, a romantic love story with a wonderful ending.

Above: Gia and me. Messina has numerous beautiful statues

I was sure that Dona Sofia missed her daughter. I found her in the kitchen and asked her about Conche. She told me that she has received letters and that the new couple was happy.

I wondered about Conche and her new life in America. What was it like? Had she become a grand lady? Did she have servants? Was he nice to her? I started to think about marriage.

Our parents' marriage was what I thought the perfect marriage paradigm. That was the husband provided a comfortable home for his wife, whom he adored, and his loving children. The wife took care of the home and the children, and understood that the husband socialized with his male friends, and not with his family. That was the way it was in Italy. Italian men like to get away to sing, to drink, to play cards, or to play bocce ball with buddies.

Almost every night Father stayed out until late. He'd enjoy his non-working time in restaurants and in bars with his male friends. He also liked going to the theater. However, on the nights he stayed at home, he had dinner with us then retired into his apartment within our home. There he had a private bath, a study and his bedroom. Mother at times visited his apartment, but she had her own sleeping and dressing quarters.

I remember one time Father had come home past midnight. I heard him open our bedroom door, and then I heard a whoosh sound when he came into our room. He had something in his hand. When he stood over my bed, I could sense his presence hovering over me, I rolled onto my back and looked up, I saw a pretty thing dangling over me; but what was it? When I got a better look, I saw tulle, sparkly rhinestones, but I couldn't make-out what he was holding. Then he dropped the thing on top of me. It was lightweight, "What's this?" I asked.

"It's a tutu," he said.

"A tutu? What's that?" I asked

"It a costume for ballerinas when they dance on stage."

A new word for me; I'd never seen the ballet, this darling thing, this tutu, was so pretty. I loved it. Gia got one too, a tutu, and she adored it.

Until this day, I wondered where he got those two tutus so late at night in Messina. They were specially made, not something one could buy off a rack. I asked myself if there were a couple of ballerina's dancing tutu-less? Such a scandal!

ʘ

Father was generous; he enjoyed giving us gifts. On each of our birthdays, Gia's was on March 3rd. At midnight, when we were in bed sleeping, he had the servants bring large silver trays of goodies into our room. We woke up to a tray of sweets and cookies, a tray of pies, and trays dried fruits and other delicious things to eat, and of course the birthday cake tray. An ornately decorated two layered cake with pink icing and white roses. He gave me flowers and then the presents. He made such a fuss, how we enjoyed our birthdays.

There was one birthday that I will never forget. It was when I turned fifteen years old, I was no longer a little girl, I had grown into a young lady. Father wanted to give me a very special gift that I would remember for years to come. During that afternoon, he took me to an expensive shop in Messina where handbags were sold. He picked out my first purse. He said it was called the pill-box purse, a fashionable Paris accessory. It was the loveliest thing I had ever seen. It was in the shape of a square box, perhaps, five inched by five inches, and four inches deep; covered in snake skin dyed red, the handle was also made of snake skin, and shaped somewhat like a half oval and attached to the top of the pill-box-box. When I opened it, the lining was a lustrous fabric of satin moiré in a soft golden tone. There was a little privacy pocket inside that zipped closed. The lid latch was made of pure gold; it was simply exquisite the way the little catch caught in the mechanism. I will never forget the way I felt when I walked home with my new pill-box purse.

The time had come for me to decide what I wanted to do with my life. Gia had been fond of acting, and Father arranged that she began taking acting lessons at the drama school. I remember her practicing her lines; she spoke them out loud to me. I was not interested in acting, what held my interest was dress design.

When I told Father that I would like to become an haute couture fashion designer, he found a lady to give me private lessons in our home. My teacher was a dress designer who at one time before the war had been employed by Coco Channel. She taught me how fabric should be cut, how to make patterns, the different kinds of stitching, and elements of design. After I had completed my studies, she presented me with a beautiful diploma. The document was ornately designed with hand painted angels, and my name written in superb calligraphy.

Now that I had learned a profession, and Gia finished her drama classes, Father believed that it was time that his daughters went out into the world. Italians parents want their children to learn other languages, to experience different cultures, these things were important for one's personal development.

Although Gia wanted to become an actress, Father was not pleased with her decision because in Italy actresses do not have a good reputation, nor are they held in high esteem. In order to please his Gia, he agreed that she could become an actress, but not in Italy. He would send her to live with his sister Agata, for whom I was named after, and her family. They lived in Long Island, New York. If Gia became an actress on Broadway, for Father, that was alright. When Father told Gia about the arrangements, she was pleased. Because Father had gone to school in New York and worked there, we had heard his stories about New York, of course, she wanted to go.

&

Good-Bye Gia

We were on the dock in Naples, we hugged each other, she said she'd write, and that she'd miss me. I saw Mother cry, but Father was stoic. He knew it was time to let his oldest daughter go into the world.

When Gia walked up the gangplank to the ship, I remembered when we boarded Captain Kelly's *The Heron* for Liverpool. It seemed like eons ago, but really it was just a few years back when we were on the voyage of a lifetime. This time when she reached the top of the gangplank and stepped onto the ship, she turned around and waved goodbye.

I was both happy and sad. Happy that Father permitted her to try to become an actress, that was an actress in New York, but sad that she was leaving.

We had been inseparable for fifteen years, we shared a bedroom, ate together, studied in the same classroom, there were the memories of living at our Grandfather's villa in Mili San Marco, we met our Irish relatives together, I remember when she got stuck in the quicksand, her riding the horse around the Irish countryside, and the changes in her character after the war. I didn't know when I would see my sister again. Mother, Father and I -- we stood on the pier until the *SS Vulcania* sailed, until we could no longer see it.

Above: In Naples, Gia, second from left, next to Mother.

It felt like forever before I received a letter from Gia. It was a good letter, I read it out loud to Mother and Father, and this is what Gia wrote:

Mi bella Tina,

First I miss you, little sister. I think about you everyday.

The voyage was wonderful. No storms like what we experienced at the Straits of Gibraltar, remember? My cabin was beautiful, first class; Father ordered so many flower arrangements, they made the cabin smell good, and look cheery. Please tell him thank you from me.

The passengers were elegant, polite and kind. There were some girls my age or close to my age and we became friends, we swam in the pool, played parlor games, and often ate together. At each meal we sat at a table that was covered with a fresh white tablecloth, there were linen napkins, beautiful porcelain plates, from Limoges, France, -- no kidding, when no one was looking I turned one over to check.

The ship had a recreation director. She arranged activities such as shuffleboard contests, afternoon swimming at the pool, and a dance band. There were some nice looking young men who asked me to dance. I danced until the band quit.

And ...there was a beauty contest. For the fun of it, I entered. There was some steep competition, but guess what? I won! I couldn't believe it. After I was announced the winner, on stage the contest organizer draped a yellow sash on me;

from my left shoulder to my right hip, it read "Miss Vulcania." Then she put a rhinestone tiara on my head (I got to keep the tiara), I was given a huge bouquet of red roses, and one hundred dollars! Wow! Everyone applauded, the other girls in the contest hugged me, and like Cinderella I became the bell of the ball, sort of. It was fun.

A day later I received a wireless from Aunt Agata; she wanted to hear how I was doing and if the ship was arriving in on time. In my return message, I told that I was having a wonderful voyage, I was eager to meet her and my cousins, and by the way, I had won a beauty contest, I was awarded a tiara, and roses -- I didn't tell her about the money. She wired back with Congratulations and that she would love to see me wearing my crown and with my roses.

When the ship docked in New York, as a joke, I decided that I wanted to make a first impression one my relatives would never forget. Since I had just won the ship's beauty contest, I decided to go ashore as a queen, as Miss SS Vulcania Beauty Queen. I wore my best dress, put on my long white gloves; I put the tiara on my head, the sash I hung from my shoulder to my hip like it was when I won, and carried my roses cradled in my left arm. When I walked down the gangplank I didn't wave flopping my hand around in the air, instead I gave a royal wave. I held up my right hand elegantly, I slightly turned my gloved hand inward then outward. What a performance! When people began to applaud, and then they shouted Hurray! Hurray! I thought to myself that I must be a pretty good actress.

From the top of the gangplank, I saw Aunt Agata, recognized her from Father's photographs. She was standing next to her daughter, our first cousin, Mary, and next to her some photographers and a reporter. When I walked down the gangplank people cheered, some applauded; I continued waving royally, I looked around, and thought who are they cheering for a movie star, a famous singer, a politician, maybe the Mayor?

When I reached land, the photographers came up to me and began taking my photograph, I posed -- I had plenty of experience; how many photos did Mother take of us when we were girls? Then I realized these people were cheering for me! Miss SS Vulcania the Beauty Queen. The newspaper reporter was from the "New York Daily News," he asked me; "Miss SS Vulcania," is what he called me, "I understand that this is the first time you've visited America, what is your impression of the U.S.?"

I looked around me, saw people grinning, some clapping their hands, I didn't have to think about it much; I took a short breath, looked at the reporter, smiled and answered his question sincerely with "it looks like America loves a Beauty Queen winner!"

Love, Gia

 CB

Hello Breasts

From the seaport of Naples the *SS Vulcania* sailed away, and with it my sister began her trip to America. It was April 22, 1950; coincidentally it was our Mother's thirty-third birthday. She said it was the worst birthday because she did not know when she would see her oldest daughter again. As far back as I can remember I had the impression that my sister was her favorite. Gia had what Mother called "angel" meaning she kind of glowed; it was her personality that drew people towards her. Furthermore, she had a striking presence, tall, beautiful, and she was intelligent.

When we were girls living in Mili San Marco, the towns' people would stare at her and at me. Some purposely passed by our home just to see if we were outside; they did this in order to catch a glimpse of us. Or when we went to church or to the market people would stop and gawk at us. It happened because there was no one who looked like us in Mili San Marco. We were half Irish and half Sicilian. Very few foreigners visited the tiny hamlet, and no outsiders lived there, except for our Mother. Gia and I had different coloring and features from the others. We were blonds with greenish-turquoise colored eyes, and in Gia's case she was the tallest girl in town; they looked at us as if we were creatures from another planet. But, Gia never let the people down; she'd approach the spectators, greet them, and even shake their hands. A natural born politician, she knew how to meet people, what to say to make one feel comfortable. People were attracted to her not only because she was physically stunning, but her personality was like flypaper: Once someone met Gia, they were stuck.

I tried to be like her, but at some point during my girlhood I gave up. Admitting to myself that we did not look like sisters; nor did we behave like siblings, actually we were somewhat opposites. While I was timid, conservative, and demur, Gia, on the other hand, was the athlete, strong, daring, outgoing, funny, and at times wild. She made the jokes, and I laughed at them; she was the apple of my Father's eye, and I was ...well, just there. She was tall, five foot eight inches, thin, graceful and moved like an ethereal muse. I was shorter, five foot three inches, my body was curvy, and I was a little knocked-kneed. The local boys couldn't take their eyes off of Gia; when she wasn't around, the boys would come up to me and ask "where's your sister?" I cannot remember how many times that happened. It wasn't until I turned about fourteen years old. Things changed when I began to feel pains in my chest area. It went on for about a couple of months. Then one morning I sat up in bed, and looked down. What I saw was no longer a little Sicilian girl; instead I had become a young woman with shapely legs, a well-rounded derriere, and "Hello Breasts!"

Above: Back row, Father and Mother, in front left me, and Gia. We are at the orchards in Mili San Marco.

It was as if they just popped out! Boom! Here again my sister and I were opposites. Gia was somewhat flat in that area. After she became a film star, she complained to me that the wardrobe ladies were continually stuffing falsies into her brassiere. When Gia was interviewed about declining an invitation to appear nude in a magazine she responded cleverly with "once a girl takes off her clothes, there's nothing left for the imagination." In her case it was true.

When people saw us together, one could see a familiar likeness in our coloring. However, after the movie studios dyed Gia's hair dark brown, it was difficult to recognize we were sisters. Gia ever so outgoing and personable; and excelling in everything she liked to do; it was no surprise to me when I found out she won a beauty contest while on board the *SS Vulcania*, but she enjoyed the competition. Unfortunately later on her competitive spirit at times conflicted with our familiar ties; what I mean there were problems between us and with our boyfriends.

When Gia left Italy on April 22, 1950, I had never before had a boyfriend. That July when I turned fifteen years old, again Mother, Father, and I celebrated my birthday in Mili San Marco, at Grandfather's estate. During the summer, it felt strange to be without Gia. I was lonesome for her company. Nevertheless, I kept busy. I liked to walk about the town, looking into shops, saying "hi" to friends, I usually ended up at the dock at Mili Marina. I enjoyed watching the sun set over the Ionian Sea.

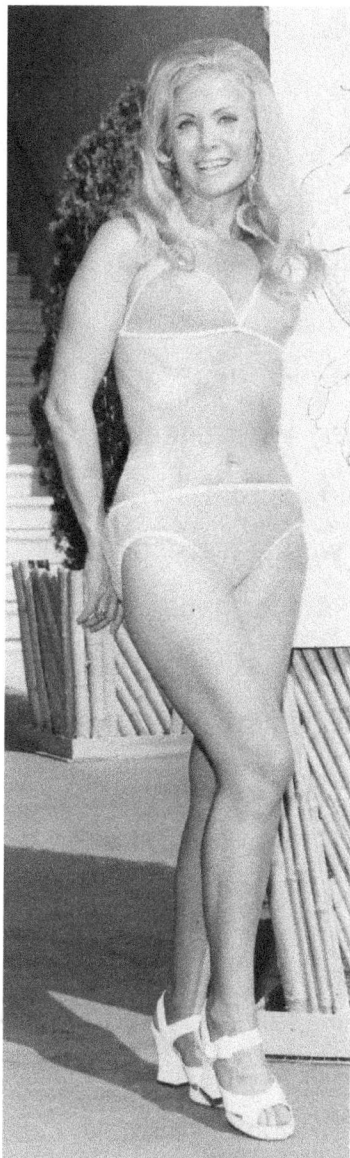

Above: That's me, Tina

On one occasion at the wharf I saw an old friend, whom I had not seen since the time Gia dived off the pier in the dark and caught an eel with her bare hands. It was Federico Silvestro. When I said "hello," at first he looked as if he did not recognize me, "It's me, Tina, Tina Scoglio," I said.

He blinked, and replied, "You've grown up."

Of course he asked about Gia, and the rest of my family. We chitchatted for awhile and then wonderfully he asked if he could call on me. I was thrilled at the thought of seeing Federico, he was quite good looking, and I said yes. During that summer, we frequented as friends, but when I returned the following spring, he asked me to go steady. Back then, in 1951, it was a very different time. Going steady meant you would not hold hands with anyone else, or be seen publicly with another. Well-bread Sicilian young ladies did not bed-down with the boyfriend, it was only after marriage, taking the sacramental vow of matrimony in the Church, would the relationship be consummated with the husband.

I was sixteen years old, and Federico became my first boyfriend. At the end of summer 1951, when it was time for my family to return to Messina, he said he'd write, and likewise I said I would too.

After I arrived home in Messina, Father began making plans for me to become more acculturated like Gia, meaning it was time that I went abroad to live in another culture and to perfect the English language. Gia had written to our parents explaining how life was living in Whitestone, New York, with Aunt Agata. She was Father's older sister by a mere ten months.

I never gave much thought that my Aunt Agata lived in New York until I started writing this story. Then I began to wonder how did that happen? Because everyone on my Father's side of the family were born in Mili San Marco, a tiny town my Grandfather used to call Mili Inferiere -- Inferiere means inferior in Italian, which was what the older generation referred to the lower part of Mili San Marco, the part near Strada Provinciale #38. The upper part known as Mili Superiore later became Mili San Pietro; it was confusing, especially because we lived on Via Giudeo Street [Street of the Jew] located more towards the Mili Marina area. I discovered that the names of the towns became Christianized after a Church was built between Mili Inferiere and Mili Superiore.

Returning to the question, how did part of the family become established in a big, elegant, and foreign city in America when we originally came from a tiny hamlet in Sicily? Big New York versus Mili Inferiere: the separation happened after my Grandmother Grazia passed away.

When she had two children the same year, Agata in January and my Father in October, 1885, she did not live long afterwards. Two years before in 1883 she had given birth to Carmella. All the children were born at home, and at the time it was not uncommon for the husband to help birthing the babies. But, in those times sanitation was not the best, and being from a small rural community, often there were deaths that went along with births. When Grandfather became a widower he was sad, but not for long.

When I was a little girl, I remember there seemed to be visitors continually in his parlor; they'd called him Don Natale, the Don was added before his name indicating him as a person of consequence. A personable man with a big smile, but behind the charming façade was a clever businessman. He was the major agriculturist in the area who owned thriving crops of olives, citrus, and lemons; but if there was a bad year in farming, Grandfather had a back up. He had designed and ordered built rental houses and apartments upon a section of his hundreds of acres of land. However, farming and real estate was not enough for him. When automobiles began to show up in Mili San Marco, he was fascinated with the machines. So much so that he invented a gas internal combustion engine. He applied for a trademark on November

26, 1928, the application was granted and the number of the trademark was #36662.

Businessman, landlord, inventor, with a big personality, he was popular with the ladies. Not long after Grandmother's passing, he married Letteria Sangiorgio. Nine month later Concetta Grazia Scoglio was born on January 16, 1889. I thought it was odd that Grandfather's child with the second wife would be named after his first wife Grazia. I'm sure he had his reasons, but what were Letteria's? Another daughter Angela was born February 18, 1890. Then a son came on July 15, 1894, he was named Salvatore. When Serafina arrived on February 24, 1898, my Father at that time was thirteen years old.

While Father and his sisters Carmella and Agata's births were not recorded with the Messina Civil Registration, Letteria made sure her four children were. Perhaps her reason had something to do with legitimacy or perhaps inheritance, nevertheless, she wanted to show that Natale Scoglio was her children's legitimate father.

When I was a young woman, I remember Father talking to me about growing up in Mili San Marco, he complained about Letteria and that they did not get along; he felt that she lacked proper comportment, culture and education. With this attitude towards his step-mother, most likely family life at Grandfather's villa was not peaceful, but on the other hand, Grandfather was a clever capitalist, and knew how to resolve problems in a universal beneficial way. For a time he had desired to expand his agriculture import / export endeavor to other countries beyond Europe and by coincidence, his brother Pasquale lived in New York.

Pasquale Scoglio was fourteen years older than Grandfather. He was born in Giardini, Messina on March 25, 1843. After he married on July 26, 1877, he and his family moved New York. Grandfather believed it would be a good opportunity for his three older children, the ones he fathered with Grazia, to live in New York; there they could become acculturated to American ways, and to learn English, and it would also be a opportunity for Letteria to focus solely upon her four children's upbringing.

An important part of Grandfather's business was exporting and for that reason he was familiar with ships. When it was time to leave Sicily with his three older children, it was aboard the *SS König Albert* where they lived during the fifteen day voyage.

The German ship first launched in 1899, was built for practicality; it was not a luxury ocean liner where passengers enjoyed a pool, parties, and good food. Instead, the crossing from Genoa, to Naples ending in New York was analogous to what it was like traveling by covered wagon in the old American West. The potential of pirates, storms, illnesses, mixed in with an international crew of dicey types, passengers of many stripes, a variety of cargo that included animals, it was a wild and wooly cargo–passenger ship which provided a voyage of intrigue as well as danger. Grandfather carried a sidearm while he accompanied his older children to New York.

The year was 1901 when Father arrived to New York. He and Agata were sixteen years old, and Carmella was eighteen. They lived with Uncle Pasquale in Manhattan, in Ward 9. Father enrolled in Columbia University, and worked with Uncle Pasquale to arrange an export / import business to and from Mili San Marco and New York.

During that era well-bred Sicilian females did not work outside of the home, and few went to university, instead, it was marriage, and having children that was important. Grandfather's oldest daughter met Paul Cicero; soon afterwards they were married, and began having children: Paul Jr. was born in 1901, Antonina arrived in 1902, Grace entered the family in 1910, Natale followed in 1914, and William became the new baby in 1922. Unfortunately, Paul Sr. passed away in 1928 and Carmella in 1931. She was only forty-eight years old.

Our Aunt Agata's matrimonial engagement ended on September 5, 1902, in Manhattan, when she became Angelo Puglisi's bride. They set up housekeeping in Queens where their first child Anthony was born in 1904, and their daughter, Maria, arrived a year later in 1905. After living twenty years in the United States, Angelo petitioned to become an American citizen, and was granted citizenship on May 1, 1936.

In 1905 Grandfather received word from home that Letteria had died. He returned to Mili San Marco to look after his four youngest children. Father, meanwhile, stayed in New York. During this time, he decided to take up the sport of boxing. Not only for the exercise, but he was somewhat of a peacock. Getting into the ring to spar meant people would be looking at him. He took good care of himself, picky about what he ate, never overweight, he exercised, he dressed impeccably, thus, boxing was an opportunity to acceptably show off his well formed body, and it was an opportunity to be seen as a potential somebody. This was important because it was a way to open doors into different New York societies.

What most likely encouraged him into the sport was the extravagance of a New York boxing event. It was a huge attraction that involved people from all levels of society, and people of all classes accepted boxers into their social circle as stars. Furthermore, the publicity of a boxing match was overwhelming. Not only did people want to view the violence, but they wanted to make wagers. It was when the Canadian born boxer Tommy Burns held the title of Heavyweight Boxing Champion. Wherever Burns went people stepped back to look at him because he was more than mortal he was a boxer. During his career of sixty-two fights, 39 TKOs, forty-eight wins, eight draws, and five loses, one of which was to Marvin Hart. On February 23rd 1906, when the Champ lost, it made more news than when George M. Cohan's "Yankee Doodle Dandy" debuted on Broadway. With all the hoopla of boxing, Pietro Scoglio, in some small way was a part of it, part of the culture of his new homeland, New York.

From sports his social circle broadened. Carnegie Hall was the "in" place to be seen. It was both a social event and a cultural affair. Father loved music, and he enjoyed singing. He involved himself into the music world when he began to write articles about musical performances he had attended. Some of his articles were published in the Italian language newspaper "Il Progresso Italo-Americano." Because of this, he was invited backstage to conduct interviews with some musicians. He began to socialize with them and for awhile he dated a violinist.

Father was an enterprising individual, when he was not boxing, or writing, or acquiring accounts for the export business, he worked at the New York Fruit Exchange as the bookkeeper and was active in the Fruit Importer's Union.

During the first two decades of the twentieth-century, 60 percent of lemons sold in the United States were imported from Sicily. The Sicilian lemons had a distinct flavor. Because of the Mediterranean climate of warm days and cool nights, coupled with volcanic soil, the lemons tasted sweet and that was difficult to find anywhere in the world where lemons grew. When the Sicilian lemon cargo landed at New York harbor, there were many importers waiting, but it was eleven men who controlled ninety percent of the lemon importation, Father was among them.

The citrus business was huge; Father earned $28,000.00 in 1910 which would be close to $700,000.00 in 2015 dollars. As you can imagine the California lemon growers did not like the Sicilian lemon importers taking away business. To create a situation where imported lemons became too expensive for the American consumer, the California lemon growers encouraged their political representatives to tax the imported lemons. In 1913, the Payne-Aldrich Tariff put a duty of $1.20 per imported box of Sicilian fruit. Consequently, the lemon importers were forced to raise the price of the Sicilian lemons.

To parry the California lemon growers' political maneuver, the New York Italians formed The National Italian Democratic League. The Republican Californian Senator John Downey Works complained to 64th U.S. Congress that the league was purposely formed "for the purpose of influencing legislation and reducing the tariff on lemons," as reported in the Congressional Record of the Senate -1916, Volume 53, Part 6, page 5877. During Proceedings and Debates, Senator Works stated that the "political organization was prompt to show its appreciation of the efforts made in the interest of the importers of foreign lemons ... the league gave a magnificent banquet at the Waldorf-Astoria and within a few days after a Democratic House had voted to remove the tariff on lemons, the chairman of the Committee on Ways and Means [Oscar W. Underwood, Senator from Alabama], who offered the amendment striking off the tariff, was the guest of honor on that auspicious and delightful occasion."

Senator John Downey Works,   Senator Oscar Underwood

At the time there were 2 million voters in the United States of Italian heritage. The League encouraged them to vote for politicians who supported Italian concerns. When the Lemon Trust of Palermo wanted to smash the citrus growers union of California, Father was involved. He along with other importers sent a letter to Congress that was read into the record.

Afterwards, Senator Works commented "I take it for granted that the tariff upon the lemons was reduced upon the theory that it was for the betterment of the consumer and upon the Democratic policy of a tariff for revenue only. ...In fact the reduction of the tariff on lemons was absolutely no benefit to the consumer. It lost to the Government about $2,000,000 year revenue. If any advantage to anyone has resulted from it, was the money gone into the pockets of the importers."

Of course he failed to mention that the Californian growers had raised their prices comparable to the imported Sicilian lemons, and they did not lower their prices after the tariff was removed.

Father developed political, social and business contacts throughout the Italian community. In the early part of the twentieth century, New York had a great deal of immigration from northern and southern Italy. The new settlers usually liked to reside in areas where there were people from their former culture. In this way, they could speak their native language or dialect, enjoyed foods from their former homeland; these things eased the feeling of homesickness. While Father's sisters married Italians, he stepped out from his culture and married a girl from Newfoundland. Although Mary F. Tobin was Canadian by birth, her family originally came from Ireland. They emigrated from Canada to New York in 1907.

In the 1915 New York census, Father's occupation was reported as a Lemon Importer. By that time he stopped boxing. He focused solely upon the family business. Due to the nature of the import / export business, he traveled a good deal. The public transportation to Europe was by ship. For the next sixteen years Father traveled from the United States to Italy or to England and back to the United States numerous times aboard several passenger ships that included the *Conte Grande*, the *Crete König Albert*, and the *SS Vulcania*. He particularly preferred the style and the speed of the Italian built *SS Vulcania*. Constructed by Cantiere Navale Triestino, at Monfalcone, Italy, and first launched on December 18, 1926, her overall length was 631.4 feet and at the cross beam 79.8 feet; she had one funnel, two masts, and reached a speed of 19 knots. Some passengers had complained that if one was on the top deck late at night, some sparks shooting out from the funnel could be seen against the night sky, and sometimes fell upon the passengers. But the unusual and unique feature of the *SS Vulcania* was she had numerous personal balconies. In first class, many cabins had doors that opened up to a private small patio with an ocean view. These first class passengers enjoyed the vista comfortably sitting in a lounge chair instead of peeking out through a porthole.

Above: The *SS Vulcania*.

When Gia was to sail for America, it was not surprising that Father booked her trip aboard the *SS Vulcania*. From Naples to New York was a thirteen day voyage. On May 3, 1950, the ship docked at pier 84 in the New York harbor. Gia entered the United States as Giuseppina Grazia Scoglio. Although her name at birth was Josephine Grace Scoglio, in

Sicily Josephine was translated to Giuseppina; it was not until she was contracted with Universal International that her name was changed to Gia.

Above: Left to Right: First cousin Mary, Aunt Agata, and Gia

Above: Left to right: Second cousin Agatha is first cousin Mary's daughter, and Gia.

Gia lived with our Aunt Agata. Her home was located at 1507 Parsons Blvd., Whitestone, Long Island, New York. Our first cousin Maria, who was known as Mary, and her daughter Agatha visited frequently.

Gia wrote to our parents regularly. She related how different and relaxed the interaction between people was in New York. For instance, in Sicily when a person meets another, they shake hands, and if they have met one another occasionally, they kiss each other on the cheek. But, in New York, it was not proper for a woman to offer her hand. The men shook hands, but not the females, and to kiss one another on the cheek, not usually unless a close friend or relative, or a child kisses the parent or grandparent good night before going to bed.

Another difference was how American women keep their homes. In Sicily, Gia was accustomed to servants washing her clothes, preparing the meals, and cleaning the house. But, in America, the lady of the house customarily did the household management, unless very rich, then the servants would do the work. Aunt Agata was not a rich woman; she and her husband had a business from which they lived, and would be considered middle class. Living in Agata's home, Gia had to help with the housework, wash and iron her own clothes, and do all of the tasks that the servants did for her in Messina. For Gia at first it was a curiosity, but quickly changed into a chore. Also, Aunt Agata's food was different than what Mother had our servants prepare. While Father insisted upon fresh food everyday, in New York although one could go grocery shopping daily, but there was not enough time in the day to shop, to cook, and to take care of the home. Aunt Agata shopped once a week, or her daughter Mary shopped for her, and kept food in the refrigerator; she prepared pasta everyday, and from eating so much pasta, Gia complained that she had gained a good deal of weight. But, the worst was she was homesick. She missed our Mother.

Mother too missed Gia; I felt sorry for her, to see her in such misery. Gia left in 1950, and two years later, it was my time to leave home. That meant Mother would be without her children. Father had arranged for me to live with the Marshall family in London. They were friends that he and Mother met in Messina after WWII. Because I was an unmarried young lady, Mother suggested to Father that it would look imprudent if I was not chaperoned to England. After all, Gia was met at the New York dock by our aunt, and so Mother chaperoned me to London.

What about my boyfriend Federico? I wrote to him explaining that Father had decided it was time for me to leave Sicily, to live in a foreign country in order to become more acculturated. On the day of my departure, I was surprised to see Federico. He had traveled from Mili Marina to Messina to say bon voyage, to watch me embark on Captain Kelly's ship *The Heron*, for England. The last moment before I boarded, Federico took my hand and gently pulled me close to his person, for a moment he looked at me and then told me to close my eyes, "Never forget me," he said. I felt his finger tips brush softly against my cheek.

C3

Gia & her King of Cool

In 1952, Mother and I arrived at the Marshal family home in London. It was grand home located in an elegant, old neighborhood. Mrs. Marshal was rather cultured. Everyday at four in the afternoon she served us "High Tea." With exquisite manners, beautiful fine china, crested silverware, and conservatively dressed -- she was the essence of a proper English lady. She had a half grown daughter, and a teenage son, his name was John. He was about my age, perhaps a little bit older. Mother noticed right away that he "fancied me."

After a month staying in the Marshal home, John gave me a diamond ring. At that Mother decided it was time we were on our own. She located an apartment; we moved in and set up housekeeping.

Because I had studied dress design, I looked for and found employment in the garment industry. That was my first job and it was exciting to be somewhat independent from my family. I used to take the tube or the subway to work each morning. Although Mother was living with me, I was away from our flat for most of the day.

During that time, almost every week Mother received a letter from Gia. Through her letters, she described life with Aunt Agata and the restrictions that she had to follow while living in her home.

After Gia finished High School, she wanted to study acting. But, the classes were costly; and Aunt Agata, who was an extremely religious woman, did not approve of her becoming an actress, or associating with potential actors and actresses. For those reasons, Gia felt it would be better if she moved to New York City. But, she had to get a job. She found work in a travel agency. Because she spoke English, and Italian, and had an outgoing personality; the job suited her. But, acting was her goal.

While working at the travel agency, she met an insurance broker whose name was Baron Francis Von Kahler. He had a connection with a person who worked in television, on a program game show. From that association Gia had an opportunity to appear on the game show. When she did, she won an iron!

After she moved to New York, she applied to Stella Adler, the drama teacher, for a place in her school. When she began taking acting lessons that same year I met Dillon Smith.

He was a sub-way ticket taker, I saw him when I went to work. At first he'd say to me "Good morning." Politely I responded in kind. After awhile he'd ask me "How are you?" Then small chitchat turned into friendly conversation. Months later he asked me out on a date.

Before we went out, Mother insisted that she meet him. When I came home from my first date with Dillon, I found her waiting for me. She was reading Gia's recent letter. She looked up and asked about my date. I said, "Wonderful. He's a gentleman." I liked Dillon, but this was new for me, I wanted to let my impressions simmer for awhile before I spoke about him "formally." To change the direction of the conversation I said, "I see you have a letter from Gia. What does it say?"

That she liked her acting teacher and the students in her class; especially a certain fellow who she thought was interesting; interesting because of how he delivers a scene in class. When Gia asked him how he makes it real, he told her that he mentally takes the scene apart, and then reconstructs the phrasing. He does it to own what he says and how it was said.

When I heard this explanation of acting, I paused and thought about it. I remembered when we went to the movies as girls, watching the actors and actresses on the screen; I never considered I was watching acting because it seemed real.

Gia described him as cute, but in a rough way. I asked Mother "What does that mean?"

She didn't know either, but thought about it then made and attempt to define it like John Wayne. Good looking, but no foolishness, a man's man.

As time passed, Gia continued writing about this fellow. In acting class he was well liked, and that Stella Adler did not accept everyone who applied to her classes, she was very particular. My sister was also picky about the guys she kept company with. Gia was not the hot-house variety of female. She was physical; liked to swim, ride a horse, to play tennis, to run, and to exercise. Her body showed it. She had well defined abdominal muscles, and sinewy strong legs, she looked like an athlete. But, she was funny like Henny Youngman. Never shy to laugh out loud and tell a one-liner. It would have to be quite a man that could keep up with her.

Gia wrote that her guy had light colored hair and blue eyes. Although he had a lot going for him, he worked as a drugstore soda jerk: that job didn't pay much. When they went out for coffee, Gia paid the twenty cents.

I was not surprised because Gia and I were contrary to each other in many ways. My boyfriend Dillon took care of our expenses when we dated. He was a sophisticated individual who wouldn't dream of having me pay for our dates. My Dillon was rather cultured, and had good manners. Well traveled, born in India, he spent part of his youth there. As a teenager, he with his family -- Dillon Sr., mother Grace, his younger siblings, John and Margaret, moved to Montreal, Canada. He used to describe to me the beauty of the Canadian countryside.

While I was thinking what it would be like to live in Canada, Gia wrote "Mother, we're so much alike. He's part Irish, like me, he laughs, charming, we smoke the same brand of cigarettes. And on the weekends we go to a place in Long Island near Aunt Agata's home where he races motorcycles. At first he did it for fun, but when the owners of the Speedway noticed how daring he was, now they pay him one hundred dollars a week to race!"

Mother became concerned about this fellow's influences upon her daughter: smoking and motorcycle racing, she wrote back asking: "Do you get on the back of motorcycle with him?"

I didn't have to wait for her response. I knew the answer. Gia liked excitement, I remembered when we were in Ireland; she'd ride the horse as fast as she could all around the farm, jumping over fences, big rocks whatever. My sister liked danger, the more the better. Now she's dating a guy whose part Irish, wants to be an actor, and races, he was the perfect man for my sister. If she married him, I thought how would they live? On the back of his motorcycle?

My sister and I were different; after Dillon and I dated for awhile he started talking about our future. He wanted to know when my birthday was. When I told him July 16th, he was startled: "Why that's my birthday!" We were both born on the same day, except he was twelve years older than me.

Gia wrote Mother about her "Cool-man," it was beatnik talk for a great guy, but somewhat of an oxymoron because when she explained about his past, it wasn't exactly cool. Growing up he was a bit of a rascal. When a teenager, he was caught stealing hubcaps; he didn't get along with his step-dad, he had been placed in a California reform school for boys because the court judged him incorrigible. At sixteen, he left the reform school and joined the Merchant Marines; but then there was something about working in a bordello that got him into trouble. Afterwards he joined the United States Marines; he got tossed into the brig for 41 days. But, not for those reasons Gia thought he was cool, it was because he was exciting.

When I heard this, I thought how similar Gia was to her Cool-man. I remembered the times she got me into trouble when she persuaded me to cut class with her to go to the movies. If Father didn't pay - off the Mother Superior, we would have been expelled from school. I thought about her Drambuie tea parties she had with her little friends, and how she hid the bottles of booze after she purchased them with Father's credit at the store. When the clerk gave her the bill she erased the word Drambuie and wrote candy. Gia and her Cool-man seemed to be like a hand in a glove, both hovering on the edge of being naughty.

After I had been dating Dillon for about six months, he asked me to marry him. I was seventeen, and impressed that this older, sophisticated man wanted to marry me. Looking back at my Mother's relationship with Father, she married a man who was thirty-two years older. Mother was like a little girl with Father; she was passive and sweet they never argued. Dillon, twelve years older than me, seemed compatible, congenial, stable, had a job, and an apartment, I thought he would make a good husband, but I was an inexperienced seventeen year old girl, I didn't know much about men. He knew I was innocent, I should have thought more about why he was not married at thirty years old, but due to my nativity, I said "yes" to Dillon. After I told Mother that Dillon and I were to be married, she thought it was good for a woman to marry young, not to have a great many boyfriends because it could dent one's reputation. Father needed to know, and he'd want to come to the wedding.

Dillon and Tina

Father gave me away on the day I turned eighteen, after the wedding, Dillon and I moved into his apartment

When I married, Father was sixty-seven years old. He had become tired of the export / import business, and wanted to retire to England. He asked Mother to find a residence for them. In the meantime he needed to return to Messina to sell the business and the property in Mili San Marco. Mother told him that she would find a home in London, but before she did, she asked Father for permission to visit Gia in New York. She explained that she was worried about her daughter's boyfriend. He seemed a bit on the wild side because he drove a motorcycle with Gia riding on the back. Then there were the parties where most likely she was drinking alcohol, smoking cigarettes, socializing late into the night, not taking care of herself. And Gia had mentioned in her letters that her Coolman had talked about marriage.

Father asked, "What's his name?"

Mother responded, "Steve McQueen."

ﾃ

Above: At Gia's wedding in 1959; L. to R, Don Burnett, Gia's new husband, Steve McQueen and Gia. It is obvious in McQueen's facial expression that he's not happy.

જી

The Hollywood Image

On February 15, 1954, *The Queen Mary* sailed into New York's harbor. The voyage from Southampton, England, by way of Cherbourg to New York had been smooth and enjoyable. Although during WWII the British military used the ship for troop transport, in 1947 it was refitted as a luxury passenger vessel. *The Queen Mary* and her sister ship *The Queen Elizabeth* were the fastest transatlantic ocean liners of the day. When Mother stepped off the gangplank onto land in New York, Gia was there to meet her, and so was Aunt Kate.

It was Eileen O'Sullivan's first time in the United States, and the first time in more than a decade that she had seen her sister Kate. When she saw Gia and Kate together, she commented to me much later their remarkable resemblance to one another. Kate had dark blond hair like Gia, and she was pretty.

Kate and Mother had grown up on the family farm located near Scott's Hill by Tahilla, County Kerry. They came from a family of eleven children. Mother asked about their sister Julia, who had also left the farm to move to New York.

Kate said that Julia had married, but her husband, who was much older than she had died; she was a widow, but not a poor one. She continued to live in her late-husband's grand house with acres of land around it. It was located in the outskirts of a tiny town in Connecticut, about sixty-two miles north-east from New York; Bethel, was the name of the town. Julia visited New York occasionally, but could not move away from the house George Edward Spier left her, nor could she sell it; it was something about a "life estate" where she was allowed to live on the property during her lifetime, but after her death, the property reverted to his grown children, the ones he fathered with his first wife. Alone, the widow lived in a big rambling house; to ease the passage of time she imbibed a bit. (Our Irish relatives enjoyed a nip. I'll tell a couple of "those" stories a wee bit further along.)

Before Mother boarded the *Queen Mary* in England, she was required to indicate on the passenger list where she would be residing in New York. I don't know how it came about but she gave her address at 65 West 54 Street, in Manhattan. The address belonged to a residential tower known as The Warwick. The interior of the building was impressive. The first floor dinning hall had murals painted by

Dean Cornwell. Throughout the building there were beautiful fixtures and artwork. William Randolph Hearst contracted to have it built in 1926, at a cost of five million dollars. It was known as a place where Hearst housed his movie star friends when they visited New York, however, the rumor was that the real purpose of the residence was a pied-à-terre for his mistress the actress Marion Davis. She was the only movie star who didn't have a room at The Warwick because she had an entire floor; designed especially for her that included a private elevator.

At The Warwick Gia moved in with Mother, who had brought with her from London four large steamer trunks packed full of clothes, hats, purses, and other lady's things. For the first month, they spent their time sight-seeing New York and visiting with Kate and Julia. While Julia lived in the country, Kate was a city girl. She had an apartment with a grand view of Central Park.

During that time, Gia continued taking acting classes. She asked her teacher for permission to have Mother accompany her to class. In that way Gia could casually introduce Mother to Steve. Of course, Mother liked him; he had "angel," as she called it, just like Gia. Mother got along with most everyone; she had good social skills, and enjoyed meeting people.

While Mother was in New York, Gia appeared on TV game shows. One in particular was "Stop the Music." Louis G. Cowan created it; he also developed the "Quiz Kids," and "The $64,000 Question." Mark Goodson became co-producer; later Bill Todman joined the production. The pairing of Goodson and Todman developed into one of the most successful TV game shows production companies that includes "Beat the Clock, "What's My Line," "To Tell the Truth," and many more.

Bert Parks hosted "Stop the Music." When Gia appeared on the show as a contestant, her looks, beauty, personality and knowledge of music overwhelmed the studio and TV audiences, the sponsors, and the producers; not only did she win the contest, but she caused such a sensation that it was reported in the newspaper:

> Some weeks ago a tall, curvy brunette, Giovanna Scoglio, of Manhattan, N.Y., stole ABC's "Stop the Music." So good was she, in fact, that she was added to the show as Bert Parks' assistant after a check with the alternate-week sponsor. The sponsor –Exquisite Form Brassieres – was understandably enthusiastic when the producers pointed to Giovanna's figure. She has a 36-inch bust. It was sheer coincidence.
> *The Salina Journal*, Sunday Oct. 24, 1954, pg 6

Gia was hired as Park's assistant on the show. Her job was to answer the telephone for the call-in contestants, and to say "Stop the Music" when the call-in contestant knew the answer.

The publicity and her appearances on the show caught the attention of Maurice Bergman who was an important individual in the New York entertainment industry. Considered a dapper fashion plate, and known for his Adolphe Menjou moustache, Bergman had one of those personalities that could have sandwiches named after him. He started in radio during the late 1920's; later Paramount hired him as head of their publicity department. In 1942 Universal International made him the eastern director of advertising and publicity. Seven years later he was appointed the executive head of the eastern talent and story department of the company. Credited for discovering Sandra Dee and connecting Frank Gorshin with a talent agent, in 1954 U - I was searching for an unknown or known actress to play the part of Mary Magdalene in an upcoming picture "The Galileans." For months the studio had been interviewing hundreds of actresses in a global search that included Rome, London, New York, Paris, Dublin and elsewhere. Bergman was impressed with Gia's looks and asked her if she would make a screen-test in Hollywood.

At this point she had no acting experience, her only theatrical exposure were game shows on television, then "bang" an offer for a screen test with a major motion picture company for a staring part in a film. She did not spend years studying acting, nor did she pound the pavement going to thousands of interviews, or did she make hundreds of auditions, it was so quick for her that she commented to me later "if it was harder for me to become a star, I would have enjoyed it more."

A few days after meeting Mr. Bergman, my sister was en route to Hollywood. She didn't know anyone in California, and she did not want Mother to return to England, she loved her very much, and asked her to come along. Mother agreed, but reminded Gia that she needed to return to London to find a residence for Father. In early 1955, they flew from New York for Hollywood,

When Gia entered the Universal International studio lot, Peter Johnson was one of the first persons she met. He had some kind of influence with the studio and that turned into a lucky break for her. Among the actresses who made screen tests at that time were Nicole Maurey, from Paris, Myriam Verbeeck from England, and my sister.

Gia made her screen-test with the actor Ray Danton, and Abner Biberman directed. The producers of the "The Galileans" liked her test, but she didn't get the part. It didn't matter because the film was later scrapped.

Nevertheless, Johnson remembered Gia, and when he saw her screen test close-up, he recognized that she had it! Not easy to describe what "it" was other than a special quality that the studio looked for. Not based so much upon acting or talent; instead it was how she looked on the big movie screen.

During the early 1950's Universal had a million-dollar talent development program where they searched for promising young talent, sometimes they chose just an attractive girl off the streets like was the case with Lana Turner. The Motion Picture Daily, October – December 1954 issue, explained U-I's position...

> With the shortage of leading name players in Hollywood, U - I has had considerable success with its talent development program ... the main reason for the lack of top name players is the unavailability of talent when a film is ready for casting. ... The U-I talent program will shortly be copied by other major studios...

After a successful screen test, new talent was signed to a conditional contract. The studio then began to build an image around the individual or in studio terms "the asset." For instance Marilyn Monroe's image became the "Blonde Bombshell" and Rock Hudson was the "perfect man." It was the perceptional image that sold movie tickets. Of course, our Mother called it "angel."

The face-shot or close-up is one of the most important elements in a movie. It is used to lure, or perhaps hypnotize the spectator into identifying with an image. It is a fantasy that the studios create to hook the viewer into buying their product, the movie.

The close-up is used mostly as a reaction to an action that may happen before or after the close-up. A good example of this fantasy is in many of Marilyn Monroe's films. The audience in a movie theater enjoys big long close-up shots of her face. Her reaction to the specific action is what the viewer feels; it is a mock transfer of Marilyn Monroe's feelings to the spectator. At this instant the viewer has a privileged personal relationship with her, as if looking into a mirror; the viewer becomes her and what she represents, such as beauty, sexual freedom, or allure. When that happens, the moviegoer will want to revisit the sensation. For the studios a successful image guaranteed future financial profits, or lessened possible losses. It was the Hollywood Star System that developed images, and controlled them.

Acting talent wasn't precisely necessary; instead it was how a person looked on the screen that the studio wanted. They contracted with almost anyone who had the photographic quality that could be turned into a studio asset. If the asset could not act, the studio provided classes, not exactly theatrical acting classes, but more like modeling classes where the asset became aware of how the camera perceives movement, and facial expressions, especially blinking during a close-up. It was prohibited, unless a scripted blink. A single little blink during a close-up could psychologically wake up the viewer and spoil the fantasy.

Not important the asset's family pedigree or where they came from because the studio invented everything. When the asset's name did not match the image, the studio changed it, such as the case with Archibald Leach who became Cary Grant, Lucille Fay LeSueur developed into Joan Crawford, Rock Hudson was born Roy Harold Scherer, Jr., and Josephine Grace Johanna O'Sullivan Scoglio evolved into Gia Scala. Her birth name was too long for a marquee, and hard to remember.

Although she had a beautiful face, her natural four front upper teeth were not perfectly straight. They looked kind of squeezed together slightly. For that tiny flaw, the studio insisted that she had those teeth capped. Her natural eyebrows were too narrow, not dramatic enough, the makeup artists created thicker and elongated eyebrows. Her sandy dark blond hair did not match the southern European exotic image the studio wanted. To correct that her hair was dyed dark brown. Finally, the studio focused more on her Italian background when they advertised her as the studio's import from Italy, and ignored her Irish lineage. Gia Scala became the new Universal International movie studio fantasy.

To test their new asset, my sister was cast in a film that stared Rock Hudson. Her first time acting and it was with a big movie star and directed by Douglas Sirk, another film great. Mother was at the filming. It must have been overwhelming for her to see Rock Hudson, and the other stars.

She watched her daughter during the filming of "All That Heaven Allows." Gia was cast as Marguerita; she didn't have any lines, and was not credited, but Mother thought Gia was wonderful. Afterwards Universal signed Gia to a contract.

Above: Gia, Rock Hudson, our Mother at the Universal International studio filming of "All That Heaven Allows."

CB

Gia Meets Clint Eastwood

When Universal International signed my sister to a contract, she became a studio employee at a salary of $100 a week. It was good money for a twenty-one year old; more than enough for Mother and Gia to rent an apartment with a swimming pool. Swimming was the sport she liked most. For $85 a month, they moved into the Villa Sands Apartment located on Arch Drive in Studio City. The two story apartment house was like many of those built during the 1950's where each residence had a view from the living room window to the communal swimming pool located on the ground floor in the middle part of the patio area. The pool created a casual atmosphere where people could meet. When she was not at the studio, she was at the swimming pool. There she got to know the neighbors. One in particular, a Universal International contract player like Gia, was Clint Eastwood. Although today he is one of the most popular actors of all times, in 1955 he was an almost unknown actor who was making $100 a week and living at the Villa Sands. Also residing at the apartment house was the beautiful screen ingénue Lili Kardell, another contract player for Universal.

Above: Lili Kardell

New to the Hollywood colony of actors, singers, and entertainers, Gia quickly made acquaintances. Not unlike our Mother, she was a sociable person. Friendly, and easy to talk to, she was invited to parties, dinners, lunches and events.

When the Italian actress Pier Angeli was expecting, Gia attended her Baby Shower. It was held during the summer of 1955, about a year after Pier married the singer Vic Damone. Gia and Pier had a bit in common; both came from Italian islands, Pier from Sardinia, Gia from Sicily, both had sisters who became actresses, they were about a year a part in age, and both died young; Pier six months before Gia.

Above: Pier Angeli and my sister. Pier's baby was born on August 21, 1955. She named him Perry in honor of Perry Como, who had given career advice to his father Vic Damone.
Notice Gia's dress, it was the same one she wore for her wedding in 1959.

Mother and Gia lived at the Villa Sands for about a year, and then moved into a duplex located at $1619^{1/4}$ North Martel Avenue. From there it was a seven minute walk to the Universal lot. Gia decided a car wasn't necessary. In an interview that appeared Sunday August 7, 1955, in Los Angeles Examiner, she explained that she didn't have a car and may not get one because walking was one of her favorite activities. Apart from swimming and walking, she also liked to paint.

She learned art appreciation from our Mother, who was fundamentally a self-taught fine-arts painter. Before she married Father, although she would have preferred to paint professionally, she was satisfied to work as a photo colorist; it paid enough were she could live from her earnings. Mother's artistic sense lent to her wardrobe panache. She had such a sense of style, it was as if she was a painter who used her body as the canvass and her clothes, shoes, and hats were the oil-paints. Especially memorable were her chapeaus. In her day, women covered their heads when they went to church, to shopping, or out in public. It was an essential part of a female's trappings. Almost all of our Mother's hats had a bird or birds attached on top. Not real birds, but manufactured bird decorations. From Mother, Gia learned style and a love of hats. So much so that my sister created her own hats; she even made the hat that she wore to her wedding.

While growing up, our Mother had a great influence upon us. She was kind, and sweet, we adored her. But, in my sister's case, perhaps because she was first-born, Mother and Gia were like two peas in a pod. They shared common traits such as a style in hats, and clothing, but most importantly it was fine-arts that they enjoyed together. They'd pass afternoons sketching and painting. It enriched Gia's life in many ways, especially when she met her future husband Don Burnett. But, that part of the story is yet to come.

Mother encouraged Gia to paint and to act. When she made a movie, the film debut was a huge opportunity for the Universal publicity department to introduce new talent. Mother proudly collected the newspaper clippings where Gia was mentioned or her photo appeared.

The second movie my sister appeared in was "Never Say Goodbye." A Universal production that starred Rock Hudson, Jane Wyman and Agnes Moorehead; the director Jerry Hopper liked Gia's looks and offered her the part of Minnie; however, again she was not included in the credits. Her former Villa Sand's neighbor Clint Eastwood also played a small role in the movie as the lab assistant named Will.

Gia along with Clint and the numerous contract players that Universal "owned," appeared in many formulaic movies that the studio cranked out economically and swiftly. U-I had absolute power over their "assets" and other contracted creative people such as musicians and songwriters. However, during this time, the Hollywood film industry started to undergo a number of significant changes. It began with

"Bernhardt in a bikini" that was what a reporter from the "Los Angeles Mirror News" called Marilyn Monroe in January 1956.

Like Gia, Marilyn Monroe came up through the Hollywood Star System. After a succession of films where she was cast exploiting her good looks and marquee value, where assembly-line directors had her play one sexy blonde after another, she realized that when her looks faded, her career was over. She needed to establish herself as a serious actress. In order to do so she wanted control over the movies where she appeared; she wanted to approve the movie story, to work with directors who had talent and personal vision and to take care of her screen image she wanted to choose the cinematographer. These were unprecedented demands from a contract player at the time. When Fox declined her request, Marilyn refused to make another movie.

In a useless effort to persuade her to reconsider, Fox tried to sour her name by generating some bad publicity about her. Didn't they realize that she was the biggest box office draw they have ever had? The extent of her popularity after "The Seven Year Itch" was unlike anything the studio had known. They had made her a star, but in their doing, unintentionally created clout for her with the movie going public; and she was smart enough to recognize her power. Fox was forced to reconsider, the studio met her demands.

However, Marilyn spanked them with a salary increase. She wanted $100,000 per film –- and she got it! In 2015 dollars that amount was about $900,000.

But, there were other reasons that Fox gave in. Like many of the movie studios in the mid 1950's their profits were declining; even though they developed new talent, and filmed movies as fast as they could. It was sometime after WWII, when movie goers started to step away from the costume dramas and the quickly made "B" movies. The cinematic shift began with the literature.

After the war, the American perceptions of life changed. New and upcoming writers like Jack Kerouac questioned the standards of the social structure, and the urban philosophy. Self introspection of one's values and views were emerging from literature and moving into film. Movies with deeper meanings such as Hemmingway's "Old Man and the Sea" were what people gravitated towards. Audiences embraced the entertaining films of the past and transcended into viewing movies that dealt more with psychologically complex characters.

Adding to the entertainment milieu of the mid-fifties was the new concept of shows made for Television. To generate audiences TV studios used the successful format of radio dramas. Weekly TV situation series of comedy / dramas of half hour to hour long segments of shows such as "I Love Lucy," "The Adventures of Ozzie and Harriet," "The Rifleman," "Tug Boat Annie," "Sea Hunt," "Highway Patrol" and so on attracted viewers. The actors, directors, and writers were paid royalties for their work and for reruns of the shows, similar to the payment format of radio programs recorded in one time slot to be replayed in other time zones. The residuals usually paid for no more than 6 reruns. At the time, it was not anticipated the potential popularity of old TV and radio shows. However, with movie reruns, there was no agreement in place to pay royalties. The Screen Actors Guild fought hard and finally won. It was agreed that movies made before 1948 were exempt from residual payments, and up to 1960, there were limited residuals. After 1970 new TV shows had no limits to the number of reruns residual payments, and movies made after that date also had different residual payments plans. But, each time an old movie played on Television, the advertisers paid the TV studios for commercial spots.

Television turned into the viewer's personal local movie theater. With that people started staying home. This cut into the movie studio's earnings. In an effort to save the studios from bankruptcy, the Motion Picture Association of America moved into action.

The take-over from one media to another was not new. From 1905 to 1915, modern cinema began with the Nickelodeon. These machines were located in storefronts. It was the first type of indoor exhibition space that was dedicated to motion pictures. In the beginning the machines were known as "peep shows." Actors did not like to appear in filmed gritty little moving images that the mechanical drama machines played. The short films were considered a low type of entertainment, similar to a freak show in the circus. Nevertheless, they were popular. However, when technology developed that advanced the length of a movie, it became the birth of the "feature film." When movies moved into theaters, the Nickelodeons faded into history.

The biggest shift in film occurred with the introduction of sound. Although there had been short films with dialogue employing sound-on-disc or sound-on-cylinder, it wasn't until Vitaphone produced "The Jazz Singer" that married the two processes. The film starred Al Jolson, and Warner Brothers was the distributor. It was the first film to have both synchronized dialogue and musical performances. Although "The Jazz Singer's" improvised synchronized talking was a little over two minutes longs, on the other hand, Al Jolson crooned six songs. Each of Jolson's musical numbers was mounted on a separate reel with an accompanying sound disc.

The film was about eighty minutes long, but had fifteen reels with accompanying sounds discs. The movie projectionist had to be nimble in order to thread the film and to cue the sound-disc correctly. In 1927 the filmed debuted to mixed reviews; the most piercing was from the "Los Angeles Times,"

> "The Jazz Singer" Scores a Hit – Vitaphone and
> Al Jolson Responsible, Picture itself Second Rate.

But, the following year, the majority of those in the movie business in the United States and in Europe, including theaters owners were converting to sound.

In the late 1920's the so called "talkie" movies were the phenomenon that turned the movie industry upset down. By mid-1950's those in the business perceived that Television was the new marvel. From 1949 when just a few thousand people owned a TV set, by 1960 when ninety percent of homes in the US had a Television set, the new media would soon beat-out the movie industry.

In 1958, Maurice Bergman saw the writing on the wall. He handed Universal International his resignation and accepted an appointment to a newly-created post of director of public affairs of the Motion Picture Association of America. His first act was to send a message to the movie industry requesting all motion picture companies for a three-year moratorium on the sale of motion-pictures to Television. This would give the movie industry a chance to recover its momentum, and to give distributors an opportunity to reappraise the situation.

However, it was Spyros Skouras who helped rescue the movie business from television. He did it with a slogan, "Movies are better than ever." In 1953 when Skouras was the president of Century-Fox, he introduced Cinemascope. This wide screen presentation of brilliantly colorful films, Television could not match. The first movie presented in Cinemascope was "The Robe." It starred Richard Burton, Jeanne Crain, and Victor Mature.

Gia came to U-I just as Television was becoming popular. The movies she appeared in before 1960, Gia was not a free agent, she was a salaried employee at Universal, and the studio kept her busy.

In 1956 she appeared in "The Price of Fear," Merle Oberon stared; Lex Barker and Charles Drake, co-starred, Gia's role was Nina Ferranti. Abner Biberman, who directed Gia in her Universal screen test, directed.

That year Universal loaned out Gia's contract to the tiny production company Monteflor, Inc., the major share holder was Errol Flynn.

CB

In Like Flynn

I borrowed the expression even though it's a bit naughty, but accurate. When one puts Errol before the Flynn, it's becomes an "a-ha" moment.

Born with an athlete's natural grace and a rogue's charm, he was a forceful screen presence, perhaps more so than any of his generation. While men admired his fast footed fencing moves on the movie screen, women envied Olivia De Havilland when the handsome, sensual, swashbuckler hero fell in love with her in the 1935 film "Captain Blood." It was his first staring role, and from it he became so popular that his cinematic image defined the era's ideal of what a man should be.

Later playing a succession of larger-than-life heroes such as Robin Hood, General George Armstrong Custer, Jim Corbett the boxer, and Spanish lover Don Juan, Flynn became something of a heroic persona of himself, that status was both a blessing and a liability. Everywhere he went, people knew him, wanted to shake his hand. He was acquainted with some of the most important, and intriguing people of the time. In contrast, his gallant cinematic image to an extent was a sensual enticement to the feminine mind. He never had to chase women.

The preternaturally handsome Australian came to Hollywood almost by accident. He had a number of jobs including gold miner, a plantation administrator, and even a newspaper stringer for "The Sidney Bulletin." He drifted into acting as an extra and gradually moving up to bit parts at the MGM studio in England. When a talent scout spotted him, he signed the 25 year old to a contract at $150.00 a week.

But by 1952, when movie audiences wanted more complex storylines than a swashbuckling hero in tights, he was downgraded to second level stardom.   At that Jack Warner canceled his contract. Without the studio's structure and revenues, in the course of the next few years he was at sea ... in many ways. Through years of reckless spending, his finances in disorder, he discovered that his business manager had been stealing from him. He began drinking heavily and gained a good deal of weight. He was 47 years old, but looked 60, even so, he was charming, an archetype of a Hollywood star. However, no American film studio would touch him. He worked in some European films, and appeared in a few television shows, but he needed to make money, big money. He decided to cash-in on his fame, and produced a couple of films with the hope that his name would draw audiences and earnings at the box.

According to Louella Parsons in her May 23rd, 1956, gossip column "when Flynn saw Gia Scala at the Universal lot, he said 'That's the girl I want for my picture "The Big Boodle." So what Errol wants Errol gets?"

Gia was twenty-two years old. At that time she had been out of high school for four years. During her high school years she resided in a protective and religious environment with our Aunt Agata. Later in New York, Mother lived with her and continued to do so when she went to Hollywood. Four years after high school my sister was no more than a girl who lived with and was chaperoned by her family, but her public image was entirely different: she was a glamorous movie star ingénue. When she went to the market or shopping, often people recognized her and stopped to ask for an autograph. The studio expected when she was away from home to have make-up on and to be dressed stylishly. Somewhat stressful to be always "on;" she could not schlep to the grocery store in casual cut-offs and flip-flops because if seen that way her movie-star persona could be damaged, and for the studio that meant lost revenues, and if discovered she could loose her job.

There were no universities that taught courses on how to deal with fame, or with famous people. Gia learned as she lived, but she had plenty of pluck. Never shy or fearful of meeting people, it was somewhat similar to when we lived in Mili San Marco. The town's people stared at us as if we were aliens from another planet because we looked different from the others in our tiny hamlet. But Gia spoke sweetly to everyone, greeted them and shook their hands. Perhaps it was a karmic preparation for her future life of a film star. She knew what to say and how to behave in public, but privately, she was still the little girl from a small town in Sicily.

When Universal lent out Gia's contract to Monteflor, Inc., the studio did not consider that they had put their young and somewhat naïve asset into an environment foreign to her and potentially dangerous. "The Big Boodle" starred Flynn, a worldly man indeed, far beyond my sister's life experiences. The script called for romantic scenes between Flynn and my sister. With his lady's man reputation, he could be a hazard to her innocence. But more dangerous was the movie's filming location: it was entirely to be made in Cuba.

Flynn liked Cuba, and began visiting the island during the 1930's. It was a place that offered him what he the enjoyed: sailing, gambling, and accommodating women. Flynn once said, "I enter a whorehouse with the same interest as I do the British Museum or the Metropolitan—in the same spirit of curiosity." While Flynn was experienced, my sister was not. She had never been to Cuba, and did not know what to expect in many ways.

Above: Publicity still from "The Big Boodle." Errol Flynn & Gia Scala

On the second Saturday in May 1956, Gia and Flynn were on the morning Pan Am flight from Miami to Havana,

Cuba. They landed at the José Martí airport, and when the DC-6 cabin door opened, Gia walked onto the platform, at that Cuba's military marching band began to play. As she stepped down on the portable aircraft steps, the actor Carlos Rivas ran up, met her half-way and greeted her with a kiss on the cheek. From the stairs he escorted her to a row of Cuban government functionaries waiting to welcome her and Flynn. She shook hands and exchanged pleasantries. Flash bulb went off as she made her way down the line. School children handed her flowers then guided her to a waiting luxury convertible automobile. Gia and Flynn were slowly chauffeured through the *malecón* – the main avenue in Havana. On one side of the street were businesses and apartment houses; on the other was the ocean. The marching band played and the children followed. Along the way Gia saw people standing on the sidewalks eager to see the American movie stars. When the vehicle approached, the spectators cheered and clapped their hands. Later Gia told me that she was so surprised and overwhelmed with the huge welcoming, at first stunned, she didn't know what to do. So, she did the only thing she could and that was she just went along.

Visiting American movie stars were good publicity for the island. Cuba's Dictator Fulgencio Batista had lived for awhile in Daytona Beach, Florida. There he observed the

American fascination with celebrities. On billboards, in magazines, newspapers, and on television -- advertisers used the images of famous people to sell products. Batista knew the welcoming parade event photos would be picked up by many newspapers throughout the United States. Errol Flynn the big movie star was in Cuba to make a movie, and he was accompanied by the beautiful starlet Gia Scala. That was news!

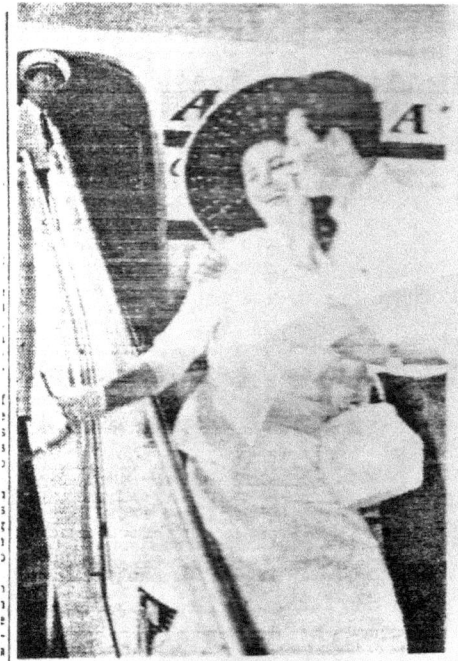

The Havana Post Cuba's only English language daily, older than the Republic—the masthead stated. Saturday May 1956. The actor Carlos Rivas welcomes Gia Scala to Cuba.

The parade was a controlled and well-planned free publicity stunt for Cuba.

The clever Dictator understood how to get what he wanted: If not intellectually, then by force. When he was voted in as President in 1940, the price of sugar was up, tourists flocked in from the United States, and the whole island had a burst of prosperity. Cuba had become the playground of the Caribbean. With its sensual rhythms of the rumba, the samba, and the unforgettable Pérez Prado and his mambo, Cuba exported to Europe and to the Americas the hottest dance bands on the planet. The island produced the best cigars, the strongest daiquiris, and the most beautiful women.

Above: Upon arrival to Cuba, Gia, Errol Flynn, and the actor Carlos Rivas were welcomed with a parade that included the Cuban military marching band, and political functionaries. Flynn dressed in white trousers and a dark jacket, is in the middle, Rivas walking next to him, and Gia walking a few paces behind them, escorted by two school girls.

After Batista left office peacefully in 1944, he moved to Florida. While there, he read disturbing newspapers reports about Cuban politics and the tourist trade. Displeased, and concerned about his financial interest in his homeland, in 1952, he returned to the island to straighten out the situation. He began a campaign for the presidency. However, a few weeks before the election, he became aware of the corruption of the electoral process. When he realized he would be defeated, in March he rounded up a group of ambitious young supporters and met at Camp Columbia, the army headquarters outside of Havana, there they organized a coup d' état.

During the time Batista took-over, the rich and the middle classes were profiting handsomely from businesses, exports, and gambling, and their lifestyle showed it. However, there was a vast underclass that camped out on the sidewalks or lived in broken down cars. University students objected to the government overlooking the poor, as a result there were uprisings and riots in the streets. To control the circumstances and any one who opposed the policies, Batista's not-so-secret police used assassination, violence, tortures, and public execution. The bodies were left hanging on trees and besides the highways as a message.

When Gia arrived to Cuba, the insurgent Fidel Castro had already returned to the island from his self-imposed exile in Mexico. He was infiltrating the countryside with rhetoric against the government and gathering followers for the purpose to overthrow Batista's régime. With guerrilla warfare in the rural areas, Castro began gaining power. It would be a difficult war to win because the Dictator had resources. Not only did he control the military and the police, but through the American gangster Meyer Lansky, he ruled gambling, and received dividends, or points as Lansky called it. Castro, on the other hand, had few means. He knew how Batista used celebrities to attract the tourists to the island. If he were to kidnap a beautiful film star, and hold her for ransom, how much could he get? It would be money for his cause and a black eye for Batista in the American press. Without knowing the potential dangers in Cuba, my sister entered a country that was on the edge of a bloody war.

However, it would take Castro until New Year's Day of 1959 to oust the Dictator. In the meantime, the Cuban government was corrupt, autocratic, whether its leaders were selected through the ballot box or not, Cuba was prosperous. In order to encourage American tourist trade, Batista did away with visas for those who stayed only 30 days; he allowed visitors to import their cars and boats. For Americans Cuba was easy living with great weather, and good fishing. Ernest Hemingway resided at his "*finca*" all year round and Flynn spent the winters in Cuba where he'd sail his beloved schooner the *Zaca* into Havana bay. On the other hand, the actor George Raft lived in Cuba not for the weather or the sailing, but for the money. Through the help of his mobster friends in the U.S., and for a percentage of the business, he became the "meeter and greeter" of the Salón Rojo, a gambling casino that was located inside the Capri Hotel.

Gambling was one of Cuba's biggest draws, but it was like a knife with a double edge: On the one hand gambling made big profits, but on the other, cheating the tourists was rampantly generating bad publicity for the island. Gambling was a free-for-all, there was no control. Cuban nightclub owners leased out their gaming rooms to almost anyone who had a bankroll. With unregulated gambling, the tourists were targeted as fair game. However, the whales, or the high roller, who visited the island knew there was only one place that had straight games. It was at the Montmartre Club, where Meyer Lansky ran the casino.

The protégé of the bootlegger Arnold Rothstein, and later business partner with Bugsy Siegel, it was Lansky who fixed things up with Batista during the 1950's so that gambling could start up in Cuba. Batista wanted Lansky to turn Havana into the Monte Carlo of the Caribbean. In order to do so he put the gambling problem in to the hands of his

Commission on Tourism, and then hired Lansky at $25,000 a year to direct the Commission; calculating for the inflation rate, in 2015 dollars it would be about $220,260.

Lansky cleaned out the cheats by moving elements of the American mob into Cuban gambling. Furthermore he encouraged hotels to have swank Las Vegas style gambling halls, and to provide luxurious large rooms for guests, classy bars, exquisite dining, and to bring in big name stars to perform in the showrooms.

From Lansky's influence over gambling and the treatment or tourists, visitors poured in by aircraft and by boat. American cars could be seen moving along on Havana streets and fancy yachts docked in her harbors. One of which was Flynn's *Zaca*. (In Samoan Zaca means peace.) She was a 118 foot schooner that he bought in 1946 for $40,000 and put another $60,000 into restorations. Originally the railroad heir Templeton Crocker had her built as the most luxurious yacht ever; her interior cabins looked as if they were designed for a monarch. Her keel was laid in August of 1929; she was fashioned similar to Canada's "Bluenose," at the time the world's fastest fishing schooner. However, after Pearl Harbor, the U.S. Navy requisitioned the *Zaca*; painted her battleship gray, and changed her name to IX-73. She patrolled 500 miles off the coast of northern California; her normal duty was a radio beacon station, but she carried two .50 caliber machine guns waiting in the wings. Crocker had spent $350,000, building her and the Navy paid him $35,000. When the war was over, Flynn bought the schooner and the first thing he did was to paint her white.

Above: The master-bedroom of the *Zaca*.

For a long time after Flynn left MGM, he sailed around the world on his beloved *Zaca*. From his travels he decided that Jamaica would become his home, but his playpen was Cuba.

He lived on *Zaca* when filming the "The Big Boodle." Meanwhile my sister and the other cast members stayed at Havana's luxurious lodging which was the Hotel Nacional.

Under new management since 1955, when International Hotels, Inc. took over -- the corporation a subsidiary of Pan Am, the principal air carrier to Havana. A year later, Meyer Lansky operated both the Hotel Nacional and the Montmartre.

The gambling scenes in "The Big Boodle" were filmed inside the Hotel Nacional's casino. Flynn played the part of a croupier who had discovered a huge stash of counterfeit money. I remember my sister telling me how shocked she was at Flynn when he was on the set because he was drinking and became drunk. He'd forget his lines and it was take after take.

Nevertheless, Flynn and Gia got along. Perhaps it was that they shared an identity with their Irish backgrounds. Flynn, although born in Australia, considered himself Irish instead of Australian. He had some Irish ancestors, but he might have been persuaded to call himself Irish because he was proud of Professor Theodore Thompson Flynn, his father, who held a prestigious position at the Queen's University of Belfast in Northern Ireland. Although our Irish relatives were from the southern part of Ireland, County Kerry, politics did not come between Gia and Flynn.

Another common interest between them was boating. Gia enjoyed sailing, and being near the water. Flynn had a lifelong interest in ships and the ocean most likely from his mother's side of the family who he had described as seafaring people.

Then there was acting, both profited from the work and the fame. But, Flynn reflected upon his super hero roles as inventions, made up, that they had nothing to do with the real Errol Flynn. "There was a fellow inside of myself," he wrote in his autobiography, "My Wicked, Wicked Ways," "who would say to me: 'You are an imposter, Flynn. In real life you don't do any of those things that you do on the screen. You are no more capable of that kind of action in real life than a choirboy.' Maybe that is why in my private life, I went ahead, consciously or unconsciously, to live such a life of reality instead of just portraying it all the time."

People who remember Flynn as the dashing swashbuckling man of action and lover of women, but there are not many stories about his kindness towards others. With total honesty I can tell you when our Mother was diagnosed with lung cancer, and had but a few months to live, it was Errol Flynn who called my sister.

He did this because when they were in Cuba aboard the *Zaca*, he asked Gia where she'd like to sail to, she said Hawaii. For years, she explained, Mother had wanted to visit Hawaii; she was crazy about the island. It must have surprised Flynn how selfless Gia was, that she put her Mother's wishes before her own.

Flynn moved into one of his other two schooners; he owned both the *Karenita* and the *Barbary*; then lent Gia his beloved *Zaca*. He supplied the captain and the crew, and he paid for what ever was needed for my sister and our Mother to have a wonderful trip to Hawaii and back to Hollywood.

When he did that for our Mother, he became my real life hero. But, I have often wondered about my sister's personal relationship with Flynn. I never asked, even if I did she would not gossip. What made me curious were the photographs I found after Gia died; photos of her and Flynn taken aboard the *Zaca* while they were in Cuba. Then there was a remark he made during an interview, he said, "If you meet a young lady ... [who] invites herself for a trip on your yacht, knowing in advance full well the risks...." When I considered that comment together with the photos, I wondered if they had shared an "in like Flynn moment?"

CB

Above: Flynn and Gia aboard the *Zaca*.

Above: Gia sailing on Flynn's *Zaca*

1957 ... a Pivotal Year

The Big Boodle" wrapped up at the end of October 1956. United Artists released it in Los Angeles, on February 12, 1957. After Gia returned to Hollywood, Universal again lent out her contract; this time it was to MGM for "Don't Go Near the Water," an adventure, comedy, romance film that starred Glenn Ford, and co-starred my sister.

One of the first persons Gia met at the MGM lot was Dore Freeman, the head of the publicity department. A key position at the studio because he knew almost everyone in the media, the Hollywood stars, the producers, and the directors. He was accustomed to dealing with beautiful and, at times, difficult stars. When stressed, actresses could become temperamental, and this would hamper film production. In order to endear himself to an actress so that she would not feel alone, to know someone at MGM to turn to in times of difficulty, Dore researched who was the star's preferred dress designer. He'd order a complete outfit in the actress's favorite color, and then arrange a publicity photo shoot; afterwards, the actress kept the outfits. This detail in which he extended himself was effective. Dore got along with even the most difficult stars.

Gia and Glenn Ford in the nightclub scene in MGM's "Don't Go Near the Water."

Notice the microphone above their heads.

Through the years, he had worked with and developed friendships with several famous actresses. For instance, Jean Harlow nicknamed him Kentucky because he was born in Louisville, Kentucky. Norma Shearer and Merle Oberon considered him a friend, but it was Joan Crawford who Dore adored. So much so that he became the president of the Joan Crawford Fan Club.

His admiration for Crawford began when he was a little boy in his hometown. At the movies it was Gloria Swanson who he ogled. "But, when Joan came on the screen in 'Our Dancing Daughters,'" he explained, "I dropped Swanson and took Crawford." He admitted the one reason he moved from Louisville to New York City was to see Crawford when she came to town.

There he worked for Western Union. "The reason I got that job as a messenger boy was that I could get autographs whenever I wanted," he explained. He remembered the time he happened to meet Greta Garbo, as Dore put it "No one meets Garbo." He saw her walking on a New York City street, went up to her and asked, "Miss Garbo may I walk with you?" She responded with, "I don't care what you do." Dore followed her a half mile until she disappeared into a department store

On the other hand, the first time Dore saw Crawford was in the early 1930's at the Booth Theater in New York City. She was with her then husband Douglas Fairbanks, Jr. Both stars were dressed in white, and Crawford carried a white gardenia. When she tossed away a cigarette butt, "I kept it for years," he said.

Because a Western Union messenger boy could go anywhere, he'd wait on the platform when Crawford's train arrived and departed. "It was my face," he said, "the first thing she saw every time she came and left New York."

He convinced the cops that it was better for traffic if Miss Crawford's car was parked in front of the theater or the restaurant that she was in. When she came out, she'd always look for him and know where her car was.

Once reporters met her arrival to ask if she planned to marry Franchot Tone, she wanted it to be kept secrete even though her future husband was on the train with her. Dore whispered to her "just say, time will tell." And she did. After that the friendship between Dore and Crawford was cemented. She gave him a gold watch and an autograph.

Crawford convinced MGM in New York to hire Dore. He began to work in the advertising department. Later in 1945, he moved to MGM in Culver City where he became head of the photographic stills department. One of his jobs was to sort through thousands of photographs of movie sets and of actors, the latter, those of whom their contracts had expired; Dore was supposed to discard their photographs and contracts. But, the photographs never made it to the dumpster. Dore took them home. The reason he did this was the photographs were taken and custom-printed by George Hurrell.

Dore admired the photographer's work because he created the first Hollywood glamour photographs. Originally Hurrell was a fine-arts painter from Cincinnati. In art class, his instructor was impressed with his paintings and suggested that he accompany him upon his return to the *plein-air* artist colony in Laguna Beach, California. Hurrell did, and was somewhat successful selling his art work. After he finished a canvas, he photographed it with his box camera, and logged it in his portfolio. When another artist in the colony saw this he asked him to photograph his artwork; and others followed. Hurrell was earning more money from photography than from selling his fine-art paintings.

Poncho Barnes, the female flying ace, was friendly with some of the members of the Laguna Beach artist colony and through them she met Hurrell. When she needed a photograph for her pilot's license, she explained that women were not allowed to have a pilot's license. Hurrell used natural lighting, and posed Poncho in such a way that her gender was undetectable. Later Poncho's friend the actor Ramón Novarro told her that he was dissatisfied with the Hollywood photographers. Poncho suggested Hurrell. Novarro showed his Hurrell photographs to the actress Norma Shearer. At the time she wanted to play the lead in "The Gay Divorcée." It was somewhat of a sensual role; the producers and the director of the film would not consider her because her cinematic image was that of a good girl, and they thought she would be inconvincible in the part. Shearer hired Hurrell. When Irving Thalberg saw the Shearer's photographs, he signed Hurrell to MGM. From the late 1920's until 1932, Hurrell photographed every actor and actress who had contracted with the studio.

Dore kept the photographs that MGM discarded. When he passed away in Los Angeles, on November 15, 1988, he had 8,030 studio photographs. It was the best and largest collection of custom printed Hurrell originals.

In 1957 when Dore met my sister, he knew from the moment he saw her that she was special. His first inclination came from the studio when they chose the ingénue to co-star with Glenn Ford in "Don't Go Near the Water." Originally, the actress Anna Kashfi was cast as the female lead. When Kashfi developed a skin disorder, she was replaced. Eva Gabor and Anne Francis were chosen for supportive roles; they were passed over for the lead replacement. This was Gia's fourth movie and she was the star. It was a meteoric rise for a new actress; from a non-credited, a non-speaking part to starring in a major motion picture. Perhaps, Gia would become Dore's new Joan Crawford.

A Hurrell-esque portrait of Gia.

Like Crawford, Gia's good looks were not the kind that wins a "Miss America" beauty contest. Don't misunderstand me, my sister was breathtaking loveliness. But there was a mystic about her eyes, exoticness in her expression; it was as if she were an old soul, incarnated for a brief moment to complete a cosmic journey. Maybe, I'm bias, so I'll borrow what William Ramage said upon meeting her at MGM's Lot 3, where "Don't Go Near the Water" was filmed. "My heart almost stopped beating when I saw her for the first time," he said, "she was without a doubt the most gorgeous creature I have ever seen." Ramage was no slouch; he was one of the handsomest men in Hollywood, and worked as a male model during the mid-1950. Dore Freeman, on the other hand, was not an actor or a model, but he knew Gia had "it." A certain kind of a *je ne sais quoi*, I don't know how to say it other than she captivated movie audiences like Joan Crawford did.

Because of Gia's potential, Dore took a special interest in her. He recognized she was a sensitive girl, and somewhat of an innocent. Part of his job as a publicist often was to arrange "dates" between actors who were appearing in MGM films. Then he'd notify the newspapers, tabloids, and gossip columnists where a certain star would be, it was a fabricated "gotcha moment."

With the upcoming release of "Don't Go Near the Water," Dore was on point. He prearranged a date for Gia and he chose the actor Earl Holliman to be her escort. In the movie Holliman played Adam Grant, a kind of adolescent Navy enlisted man, he was young, good looking, and charming. They made a believable couple.

Above: Earl Holliman and Gia, on a publicity date.

Left to Right: Eva Gabor, Ann Francis, Earl Holliman, Gia, Glenn Ford. Everyone was looking at the bloomer flag except Gia. In the movie her love interest was Glenn Ford, but in the photo she's smiling sweetly at Earl Holliman.

However, in one of the publicity stills, all the cast members were looking at the flag, except Gia. She was looking and smiling at Earl Holliman. From that photographic "blooper," I assumed that Gia liked Earl more than a just a cast mate.

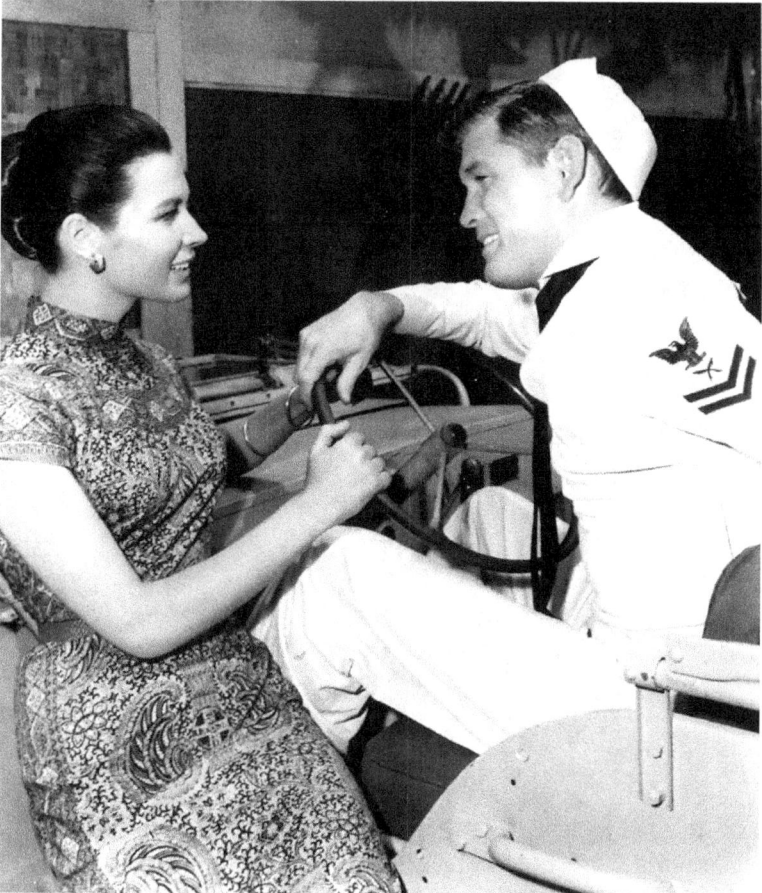

Above: Gia and Earl Holliman, on the set of "Don't Go Near the Water."

At the debut in December 1957, Gia seemed happy and congenial, shaking hands and talking with the public. Photographers took pictures of her smiling, but I knew she was acting. She felt like I did terrible because our Mother passed away six weeks prior to the movie opening.

Above: Me and Dore Freeman at the Beverly Wilshire Hotel, accepting an award for a British actress.

When the film debuted Keenan Wynn showed up and so did Don Burnett. Although Don was not credited in the film, the six foot three inch tall Rock Hudson look a-like, he played Lieutenant Hepburn in "Don't Go Near the Water." The slap stick comedy scene where the officers were attempting to build a clubhouse, Don was thrown from a ladder while he had a large roll of tar paper on each shoulder. He fell into a hole, and passed out, he made it look real.

Above: Keenan Wynn and Gia Scala

During the filming was when Gia met Don. At first nothing clicked between them. Perhaps he was busy with someone else as Walter Winchell reported in June 1957, "The MGM actors Lori Nelson and Don Burnett are singing in rhythm."

In 1963 Gia explained to the gossip columnist Hedda Hopper: "I was doing a picture at Metro [MGM] and he [Don Burnett] was under contract there. We met at the studio but

193

didn't date right away. I went to Europe for a picture and began to date him when I came back."

Above: Don Burnett, Gia, Glenn Ford, and MGM's Leo the Lion, publicity for "Don't Go Near the Water."

The movie she went to film in Europe was "Tip on a Dead Jockey." The outdoor scenes were shot in Spain and the indoor ones at the MGM studio in Culver City. Robert Taylor, Dorothy Malone, Jack Lord, and my sister starred. The director was Richard Thorpe. It was released in New York, on September 6, 1957.

AEROPUERTO-MADRI - Bracheto 19...

Above: Gia arriving to Madrid Spain to film "Tip on a Dead Jockey."

Above: Dorothy Malone, Jack Lord, and Gia, from "Tip on a Dead Jockey."

In 1957 Gia worked in four pictures. Universal, used her in one film, where she played Vicki Dauray in "Four Girls in

Town." The movie starred Julie Adams, and handsome George Nader.

Henry Mancini had joined the Universal music department in 1952; often he'd visit movie sets to get an idea of the music that he needed to write for the film. He had heard about the new Italian ingénue. When he stopped-in at the "Four Girls" stage, and saw Gia, "Wow! Ciao Bellissima!" he said. Although Henry was born in the Little Italy section of Cleveland, his father had immigrated to the United States from Abruzzo, Italy. After meeting Gia, Henry was so inspired that he wrote a tune for my sister and called it "Cha Cha Cha for Gia." It was used in the movie even though Mancini was not credited. Later in 1958, Tommy Dorsey and his band recorded the song, and other musical groups have also played it.

The actor John Gavin also had a role in the movie. Later when he was filming the short lived television western series "Destry," he commented on the situation at Universal during the decline of the film industry with, "When I came to Universal, they were making 40 pictures a year. I walked through the gate, was given a contract, and immediately the number of pictures dropped to eight or nine a year." He wasn't complaining because he was "given good roles with scope and breadth. But I wish," he continued, "I could have been put in 40 or 50 roles before making my 'first' picture. ... Doing the TV series was like putting the cart before the horse."

That same year Gia's contract was lent to Columbia for "The Garment Jungle." The director Robert Aldrich had no problem with the selection of the seasoned actors Lee J. Cobb, Richard Boone, and Joseph Wiseman, however, he took exception to use some of the younger actors forced on him by the president of Columbia Pictures Corporation Harry Cohn, in particular Gia Scala. Aldrich suspected the reason Cohn hired her; it was well known throughout the movie making industry that Cohn demanded sex from female actresses in exchange for a part in a movie.

Gia played the fashion model Theresa Renata. Although the Production Code was still in effect, during the scene where Gia danced, and twirled around, as her skirt flew up the camera moved in for a close-up of her long naked legs. It would seem as though that the Production Code would disallow that type of nudity. For instance, after the Code went into effect in 1932, the flapper-like cartoon character Betty Boop had to change from wearing a short dress into an old fashioned housewife skirt. Meanwhile Gia could fling up her skirts with impunity. Nevertheless, the risqué cinematography did not hamper the film from receiving a Production Code certificate of approval.

Her participation in the film was overshadowed by the aggression and the violence of the rackets in the New York garment industry. Harry Cohn, most likely due to his ties to the mob, preferred that the movie's focus was upon romance. When Aldrich disagreed, Cohn replaced him with director Vincent Sherman.

CB

In August of 1957, Gia wired me in London. Worried about our Mother, she explained that from the time she had returned to Hollywood from filming "The Big Boodle" in Cuba, she noticed Mother coughing frequently and had lost weight. Mother, on the other hand, told her not to worry that it was the sniffles or a cold; it would take it course then go away. She did not want to see a doctor. The coughing went on for months. Gia became adamant that she must go to the doctor. When she did, she was told that it was carcinoma of the lung; Mother had but a few months to live.

Before I arrived to Los Angeles, Gia was already distraught about Mother's condition. She had become friends with the doctor who was taking care of Mother. On August 1, 1957, while she was driving home from having a drink with the doctor, her car went out of control. The newspapers reported the following:

GIA SCALA FACES DRIVING CHARGES
Pacific Palisades, Calif.
Starlet Gia Scala, 21, was booked on suspicion of drunk driving early today when her imported sports car crashed in Pacific Palisades.
The Irish-Italian actress escaped injury from the mishap in front of the home of Martin Prasky at Chautauqua Boulevard near Pacific Coast Highway at 2:15 am.
Officers said she failed an intoximeter test.
"I just had a couple of glasses of champagne with the doctor who is treating my mother," the actress told police, who booked her at city jail.
She was released at 8:10 am on $263 bail and ordered to appear in division 33 of Municipal Court at 1:30pm tomorrow.
The blue-eyed beauty recently had a role in "The Garment Jungle." She carried $392 in her purse.
Officer J.R. Ide of West Los Angeles police division said Miss Scala's Austin Healy left 124 feet of skid marks on the pavement before it bounded on the steep grade and struck a plant in front of the home.
Miss Scala, 1616 ½ No. Martel Ave., Hollywood, was booked under her legal name of Giovanna Scoglio.
"I was not drunk," she insisted.
Police quoted the actress as saying the doctor she had seen told her that her mother had only a few months to live.
The Citizen's News, August 1, 1957.

In late August I arrived to Los Angeles; the columnist Louella Parsons wrote the following:

> Gia Scala's sister Mrs. Agatha Smith, has arrived from London because of the grave illness of their mother, Mrs. Eileen Scoglio, in a local hospital.
>
> *Cumberland News,* Monday, August 26, 1957.

It was the first time in four years that I saw Mother and I was shocked. She was so very thin, almost transparent; she looked as if a slight gust of wind could float her away. Nevertheless, she was happy to see me, as always she was the sweetest and kindest person anyone could ever imagine. She had a zest for life unlike anyone; where she got that I don't know because growing up must have been difficult.

She was born on April 22, 1917, at home, in a house constructed of stones that had a thatched roof; it was rental house number 3 in the town land of Derreenaclough, within the Barony of South Durkeron, County Kerry, the poor law union of Kenmare, Tahilla, it was in the southern part of Ireland not far from the coast. Her father Cornelius Sullivan was a farmer, and his wife Johanna took care of their eleven children; the widow Mother Sullivan resided with her son's family. In all there were fourteen people who lived in the two room stone farmhouse, but the two cows Cornelius owned each had their own barn, and a separate calf-house for the bovine younglings.

Cornelius, Johanna, and Grandmother Mary Sullivan -- none of them could read or write, but they spoke the English and the Irish, as they called it. The oldest daughter, Kate, was the first to become educated. She could read, and write in both languages. All the other children only learned to read, to write, and to speak the English.

Johanna was fifty-four years old when she had her last child; Lizzy was born in 1911. Not less than thirteen years later, Cornelius passed away -- only sixty-three years old in 1924, and that was the year everything changed for the Sullivan family.

Tahilla, a brutally rural area, where family farms were spread miles and miles apart over the 496 acres of Derreenaclough; there was no work for the Sullivan children. Most of them left the farm to find jobs in other places. Kate went to New York, Julia followed as did Michael, and Joan, who was called Hannah when a child. While Denis and Lizzie stayed on the farm with their widowed mother, Cornelius Jr., Mary, Nora, Bridget and Ellie, who no longer wanted to be called by her girlhood nickname, preferred Eileen, moved to Liverpool.

Of course that was where our Mother, Eileen, met Father. He must have impressed her with his courtly Sicilian manners, his elegant Rudolf Valentino-esque style of clothing, and his posh semi-detached home located at 61 Brideoak Street, Cheetham. Meanwhile, she lived in a tenement apartment house at 103 Bignor Street, Cheetham; she was an Irish country lass with big turquoise colored eyes and dark auburn locks who was unaccustomed to city dandies, and indoor plumbing; with little worldly knowledge, she married Father on September 16, 1933. Their daughter Gia was born six months later.

Above: Marriage Certificate of Pietro Scoglio and Eileen O'Sullivan

A happy marriage, indeed, they never quarreled. Mother was somewhat like a little girl with Father, speaking softly and sweetly, always with kind manners. But, there was a secret between them that Mother took to the grave. It was fifty years later I discovered the mystery. I felt it would be inappropriate to disclose it blatantly, but a close reading of this book shall give the reader a moment of "aha!" reality.

CERTIFICATE OF BAPTISM

Above: Uncle Denis and Aunt Lizzy were Gia's God-Parents.

During the last months of Mother's life, Gia could not get out of the contract for "Ride a Crooked Trail." A western filmed at Universal starring Audie Murphy, Gia co-starred. At home my sister was by Mother's bedside almost all of the time, but when her breathing became terribly labored, she was hospitalized. When that happened, it became somewhat of a relief for Gia because she knew that Mother was well cared for in the hospital while she was at work.

I had never seen the inside of a movie studio; I asked Gia if I could go with her to the set. I remember walking through the cavernous place to her private dressing room towards the back. Inside it was nice, there were things to drink, sodas, juice, and some snacks. I could hear someone laughing loudly; it was the people next door. Sounded like two women yakking up a storm. Gia said it was Audie's friends. When it was her cue to be on the stage, we stepped outside and found Audie was leaving his dressing room at the same time.

Gia turned to me quickly and whispered that Audie was a little uneasy with her because they had never met before the movie; but on the first day of filming, Audie had to kiss her.

Gia introduced me as her little sister. I found him extremely polite, and respectful. I could not imagine that he was with those noisy ladies, but I could see in his expression, that he "liked" Gia.

Every evening after work Gia went to the hospital. She'd stay until the morning. On one night in particular we were at Mother's bedside, Gia was exhausted from working long hours. She hadn't slept in days and said to me, "Let's go home, I must get some sleep."

We arrived at the duplex on North Martel Avenue around three in the morning. Gia took the telephone off the hook. I was worn out from the stress and worry about Mother. I fell into a deep sleep. Then I was awoken with the sound of loud banging on the front door. When I opened it Dore Freeman was there. He said, "I've been trying to call for about an hour. The phone was busy. I decided to come by. It is your Mother, she has died. I'll take you two to the hospital."

On October 26, 1957, Mother left us. She was buried two days later; coincidentally it was Father's seventy-second birthday. He did not come to the funeral, and their secret did not leave the graveyard.

Above: Gia, talking of the telephone, and our darling Mother sitting on the davenport at the duplex on North Martel Avenue.

CS

Through Difficult Times

Devastated, Gia was overwhelmed with grief. Mother's death seemed to paralyze her intellectually and emotionally. More than heart-sick, she was soul-sick. She was a ship without a rudder. Mother was my sister's rock, her best friend, her confidant, and upon whom she modeled her life. When Mother left, my sister became numb.

Because Gia worked a great deal, she did not have much of an opportunity to make friends with individuals outside of show business. However, those whom she knew from work began phoning and visiting. How kind the Hollywood movie people were to her. Henry Mancini came to the duplex; after he offered his condolences, he began to sing, and then he was dancing around the living room; when he started jumping up and down on the sofa while singing a silly song, Gia laughed so hard at his antics. With the endorphin high, she felt good for awhile.

Above: Henry Mancini and Gia.

Charlton Heston called to set up a date to play tennis with Gia. However, a few days later when he arrived at the duplex to pick her up, she told him that she was not in the mood to play tennis. Disappointed, but he understood.

I left Hollywood to return to London. By plane from Los Angeles to New York, then I took the *Queen Elizabeth* bound for Southampton, England. I arrived home to 121 Goldhawk Road, in London, on November 26, 1957. Physically exhausted from the journey, and emotionally drained, later when I wrote to Gia telling her about my trip home, and asking how she was, she replied that Doris Day invited her to a Christmas tree decorating party.

Above: Gia, left, at Doris Day's Christmas tree decorating party.

Gia was contracted to appear in "The Tunnel of Love." Filmed at the MGM studios, Fields Productions and Arwin Production produced the movie, the latter company Day and her husband Martin Melcher owned. The film starred Day, Richard Widmark, Gig Young and my sister. The dancer Gene Kelly was the director. Although Gia began filming "The Tunnel of Love" late 1957, it didn't debut until November 21, 1958.

On the movie set, there was a good deal of dead-time, where actors were waiting for the next shot to be set up. Gia's favorite pastime was to sketch.

Above: Richard Widmark posed for his portrait sketch by Gia.
Below: A scene from the "Tunnel of Love"

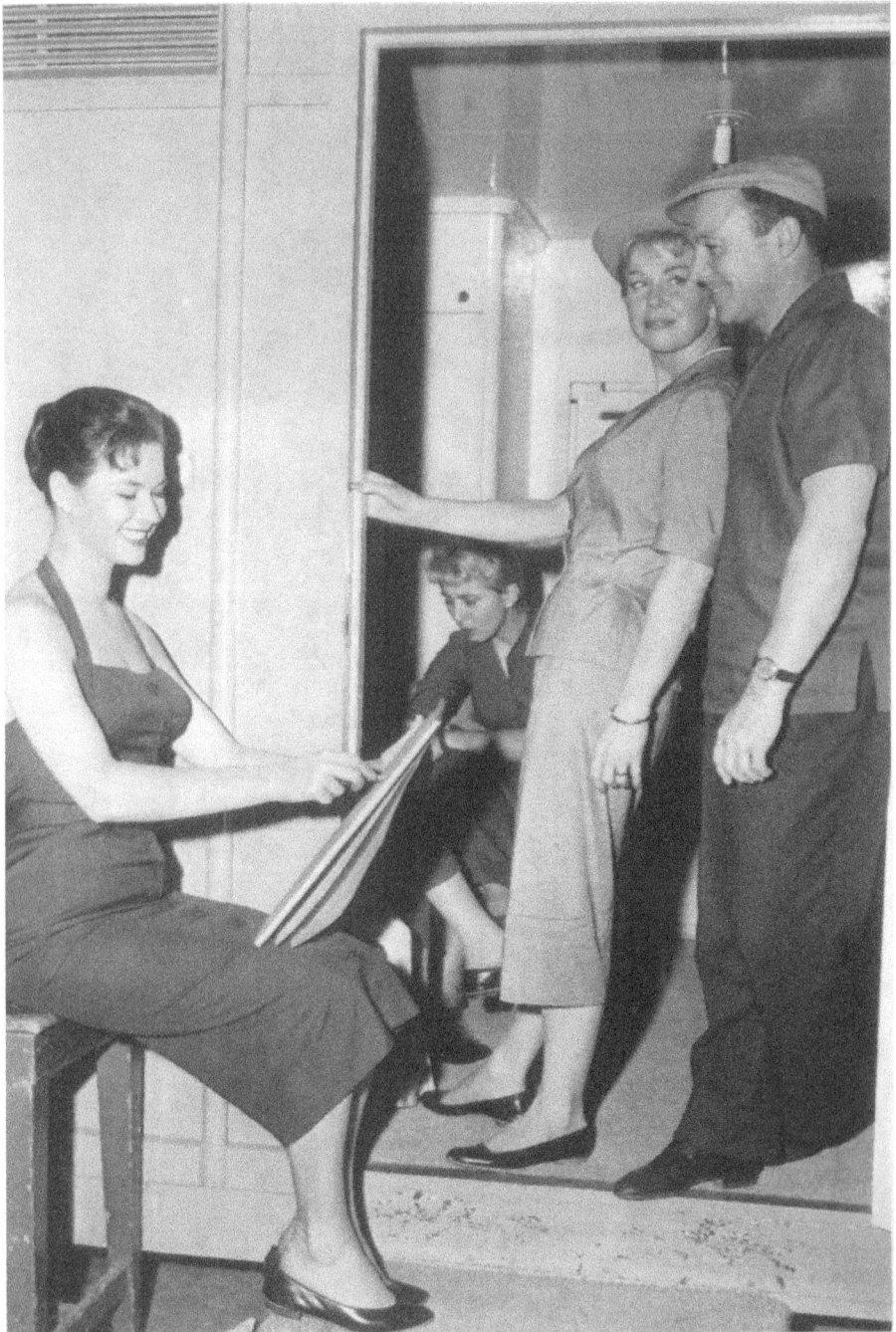

Above: Gia sketching, Doris Day looking at Gene Kelly

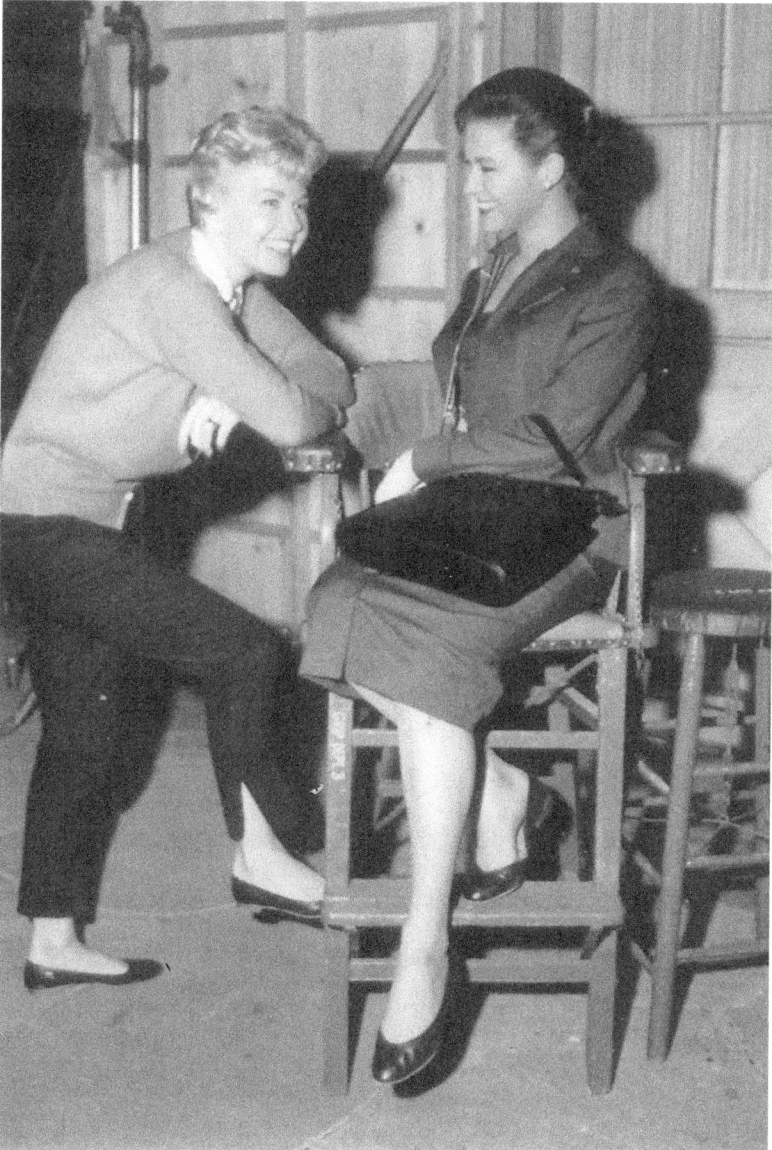

Above: Doris Day and Gia on the set of "The Tunnel of Love."

Above: One of Gia's paintings

As far back as I can remember my sister painted pictures. Portraits were her favorite genre. Gia had asked me a couple of time to sit for her, but I never did. After she died I regretted that I didn't take the time to have her paint me. Mother and my sister, I recall many times watching them each with their easel or sketch book, working on an art project.

When Gia left Sicily for the United States, she was happy to go to America, I could not have imagined that she would ever return to live in Sicily, or would I see Mother and her painting together again. But, Mother in some way knew that they would be rejoined in America.

"I dreamed of America since I was little," Gia told Hedda Hopper, "because every time I cried, Mother would soothe me with 'don't cry darling, tomorrow I'll take you to America.'" (*Chicago Tribune*, N.Y., 1961)

In February 1958, Gia became a US citizen. When she traveled to London to film "The Two Headed Spy," she carried a US Passport

௫

The Bridge

GIA SCALA SAVED FROM THAMES
Man Balks at Suicide Attempt
LONDON
A taxicab driver pulled young movie actress Gia Scala from the parapet of Waterloo Bridge high over the river Thames early Tuesday. The driver, who had driven the 22 year-old Irish-Italian starlet from her apartment, grabbed her as she teetered on the stone parapet of the bridge, and summoned the police.

A police car took Miss Scala to Bow Street Station where she refused to give her name and spent the rest of the night at the station, apparently in a state of partial shock. Tuesday morning she was taken home by her father. To later inquiries her father said she was "very tired and is now sleeping."

Neighbors of the actress said she had gone out the night before with a dark "Greek-looking" man and returned alone. An argument was then heard in the apartment she shared with her father.

Miss Scala whose real name if Giovanna Scoglio, was born in Liverpool. Her father is an Italian and her mother Irish. She went to Hollywood

three years ago to make movies, and in March of this year she returned to England to film "The Two Headed Spy" with British star Jack Hawkins. Last month she went to Greece to make a movie with Robert Mitchum, "The Angry Hills."
Independent, Long Beach, California, August 6, 1959, pg. 3

The news was shocking. I knew Mother's death effected Gia a great deal, but to jump off a bridge was cockamamie, I could not imagine that she would do such a thing. I asked myself what were the circumstances of her actions. The news article mentioned a Greek-looking man. Perhaps it was Plato Skouras. He had followed his father Spyros Skouras into the movie making business. While Spyros was the president of 20th Century-Fox, Plato started his own film production company. Perhaps Plato invited Gia to dinner to discuss a forthcoming film where she might star. However, according to the article, Gia retuned home then had an argument. It had to be with Father. Strict and at times stern, he was nothing like our sweet Mother.

When Father allowed Gia go to America, he thought she would finish school, find a fellow, get married and have children like a good Sicilian girl. He paid lip service to her intentions of becoming an actress. Never had he imagined that she would become a movie star. After all, she had a distinct European accent when she spoke English. When she went to America she had no connections with show business people, and there was steep competition between actresses. His Italian mentality concerning actresses was that they were naughty girls. I asked myself why he thought that way. Had he personally known an actress? Then, I remembered when Gia and I were girls, late one night when he brought us tutus. He woke us up with these lovely gifts; it must have been past midnight. Where did he get them?

Even if he at times was a rascal that didn't mean he wanted his daughters to be like him. But, he forgot that his children carry his genes. Did he believe that we would be different from our parents? He must have been terribly troubled when Gia became an actress.

In his mind his little girl was unmarried, un-chaperoned traveling to Greece to film a movie with Robert Mitchum. Father had seen Mitchum's movies and liked his acting, but he also knew he was a man, one of reputation. For Father, a girl's most important event in life was to be married, perhaps he said to Gia "look at yourself, traveling all around without a chaperone, working as an actress, who would want to marry you?" Ouch!

She must have felt worthless; it was late at night, she was tired, not thinking straight, Father disgusted and ashamed of her lifestyle, Mother was dead, she had no one. It was a dark place. She had to get out of the apartment.

Waterloo Bridge at one time was called the Suicide Bridge. Decades past, an American daredevil was attempting a dangerous feat on the bridge when the rope slipped, in front of hundreds of spectators, he inadvertently hung himself.

Gia Scala and Robert Mitchum on the movie set in Greece while filming "The Angry Hills."
Robert autographed the photograph to Gia with: "But grandmother, what big eyes you have!! Love, Bob."

In a scene from "The Angry Hills," Gia Scala and Robert Mitchum; Robert Aldrich directed.

Even though my sister had problems with Father, the movie critics did not. One of whom, Connie Conrad of the *Pittsburgh Press*, reported February 1, 1959, that Gia Scala "only recently delighted movie audiences with a slick comedy performance ... in 'The Tunnel of Love.' Now, in 'The Angry Hills,'... Gia shows you the other side of the coin. ... She has a role that is strictly dramatic. And audiences who laughed at her quips in 'Tunnel' will be reaching for their handkerchiefs in the scene in which Miss Scala has to cry."

Gia, second to the left, with friends in Athens Greece.

After Gia left London for Hollywood in late summer of 1958, Father returned to Sicily. He was about to turn seventy-three years old, he had sold his business, Mother had passed away, and his children were grown.

He settled in Taormina, Sicily, a small beautiful seaside vacation hamlet tucked into the hills that overlooked the Ionian Sea. It was no more than thirty miles south from Mili San Marco, the place where he was born. He moved into a home that had a view of the shoreline and the town.

In the fall of 1958 I visited Father. When I arrived I remember colorful bougainvilleas growing everywhere, wild flowers covered the hillsides, and the sea air had a fragrance that uplifted the spirit, a lovely place to pass one's senior years of life.

Father had rented a suite for me in the most intriguing hotel, it was not a modern building but one that was built like good red wine should taste: memorable.

He accompanied me to my rooms on the second floor. They were spacious with tall ceilings; it reminded me of our home in Messina. When I opened the double French patio doors, on the balcony was a magnificent display of the most beautiful flowers. Father had the town's flower grower decorate every inch of the balcony with flowers. It was a breath taking sight, the fragrance heavenly. Father was splendid, thoughtful, and detailed. I adored him.

Above: Father, later in life.

ଅଟ

The Hollywood Hookup

I knew I had to leave Italy when I was 15 or 16," Gia commented to the columnist Vernon Scott of the *Lubbock Morning Avalanche*. "Otherwise," she explained, "I would have been married at 18 and settled down to being a housewife. You have no idea how little of the world the average Italian housewife ever sees. Her whole life is lived within a few miles of the place where her husband lives." Friday, January 13, 1956, page 29.

My sister liked excitement and fun. For Gia to marry young was like yoking a racehorse to a plow, but that was before Mother passed away, afterwards, she changed.

଼ଓ

Upon returning to Hollywood from London, Dore Freeman was not impressed with the negative publicity his favorite ingénue received from the incident at the Waterloo Bridge. He recognized that Gia was distraught from Mother's passing. She was alone in Hollywood, no family for support. Dore thought the best solution for her was to marry.

As a professional publicist he hooked-up stars for publicity dates, why couldn't he do the same for a real date. He remembered when Gia told Vernon Scott in 1957: "My dates are limited," she sighed, "I don't have time for them. Besides, I left Italy because I didn't want to marry young and I still feel that way."

But she did have time for Arthur Lowe, Jr., whom she dated, even though he was going steady with Eartha Kitt. *The Nevada State Journal* scooped that gossip for the Sunday edition, Feb 6, 1955, page 4.

And then there was the note that appeared in *The Record-Argus,* Friday, November 23, 1956, page 1:

> The beauty sharing a table for two at Loujon's with film executive Charles Simonelli was Gia Scala of the Celluloid's.

What was Gia's type of man? An executive type? No, too starchy for Hollywood debuts, the red carpet, and interviews. He had to be in the business, an actor preferably a very handsome actor, an MGM actor. Tall, yes, necessary because she was 5 foot 8 inches in her stocking feet; with 3 inch high heels, she tipped 5 foot 11. He had to be at least 6 foot, and a few years older than she because it was not fashionable at the time for a female star to date a younger man; and never married, yet settled down. That would be a tough one to fill. A good many young actors were outrageous playboys, or heavy drinkers, or something was wrong.

He remembered Hedda Hopper's January 1958 comment about MGM's Don Burnett and Leslie Nielson that they were "pat investments." Leslie was a good actor, but Don was better looking. Could Don be a husband candidate for Gia?

Don Burnett

Don was about six foot three inches in height; his body was strong, well-formed and athletic. He had a loving, respectful nature; it was not difficult to recognize that Don came from a good family. Dore knew Gia missed her Mother and needed to be around caring people. Another positive aspect was that Don's mother Rose was Irish. Although she was born in Toronto, Canada, her parents emigrated from Ireland.

His father Albert John Burnett came from England, at Kent. When he was a youngster Albert moved to Canada with his family. He lived with his widowed mother until World War I when he joined the Canadian Over-Seas Expeditionary Forces. After the war, he returned to Toronto, and started working as a Laboratory assistant, but his job didn't fulfill his passion in life. He wanted to work in the field of art.

After Albert found a job as an artist for a commercial concern, he gradually worked his way up in the company to become the director of the art department.

Albert and Rosine Kathleen Forhan married on December 22, 1923, in Toronto, Canada. Later the young couple immigrated to Los Angeles, California, where Albert had a job waiting for him in the art department for a carton company. They lived at 1724 Easterly Terrace, in a small home within a middle class neighborhood.

Don was their first child. He was born in Los Angeles, on November 4, 1930. His brother Norman came along on February 23, 1933; and Mary was born on Christmas Day 1934.

Don seemed like a good match for my sister. But what convinced Dore of their compatibility was that they shared a passion for art. Both Gia and Don learned to paint from one of their parents.

Don lived in Malibu, he and the actor Rod Taylor shared a house at 1495 ½ Pacific Coast Highway. All through the late 1950's it was a different era, gossip like which Don's friend Rock Hudson endured, didn't apply to him.

He and Rock met during the time Rock was divorcing his wife Phyllis Gates. Rock had become disillusioned with marriage, his biographer Sara Davidson described the situation as:

> Rock's relationship with Phyllis began to deteriorate after "Giant." In Rock's view, Phyllis changed when she became Mrs. Hudson. She went on buying sprees, and she fired Rock's housekeeper ... who had been with him since his first days at Universal. Phyllis became more possessive; she would call the Studio and monitor Rock's movements through the day. Most important, Rock felt, she was no longer warm and fun-loving; she was constantly picking on him.
> *Rock Hudson: His Story,* Rock Hudson & Sara Davidson, 1986, p. 103

When Rock moved out of the home he shared with his wife, he went to Malibu. There he lived in a house that was built on wooden stilts over jagged rocks where the ocean waves splashed beneath. Gradually he got to know some of the local residents, and fell in with a group of guys who worked in the movies as stuntmen and bit part actors. Among them were Rod Taylor and Don Burnett.

Don explained "life with Rod and Rock was macho and physical. We went swimming in the ocean without wet suits all year round. We did a lot of running in the Malibu hills, then came down to the beach and jumped into the ocean. We went sailing, and scuba diving. ...There was heavy drinking, but the sexual stuff was private."

Similar to Gia, Don was a sociable person. Although he liked to go out at night with "some of the guys," they went to bars in rough neighborhoods just "to get in fights now and then." (Hudson & Davidson, 1986, p. 121.)

For my sister, Don was exciting, handsome and eligible husband material. And for Don, to be dating a beautiful, athletic, and daring girl like Gia, well... it was kismet. Furthermore, both were on track to become major stars.

After Don finished filming the successful T.V. drama, "Northwest Passage," in March 1959, Gia and Don decided to marry.

On August 20, 1959, The Citizen News, page 3, reported

TOMORROW THE'LL SAY 'I DO!'

Actress Gia Scala and TV actor Donald James Burnett, 28, Malibu, are shown as they obtained a marriage license yesterday at Santa Monica. They plan to wed tomorrow and to take a honeymoon trip to New York City. The actress' real name is Giovanna Scoglio.

ॐ

The Wedding & Reception Photo Album

Gia becomes Mrs. Don Burnett , August 21, 1959
I do.

Gia thinking, should I or shouldn't I?

Married in Los Angeles Superior Court Judge Burnett Wolfson's chambers.

Gia gets a kiss from the Judge. Look at Don's expression.

Hedda Hopper, Don, Gia, and director Richard Thorpe

Harriet Aldrich, director Robert Aldrich's wife was the witness.

The Reception

Right: Director Robert Aldrich, Don and Gia

Actor Russ Tamblyn congratulates Gia

Steve McQueen toasts the new couple

Above: Steve McQueen, Don Burnett, Gia, and Neile Adams, Steve McQueen's wife.

ⓒ

A Marriage in Haste?

Gia and Don

Only 12 months before her August 1959 wedding, Gia was about to jump from the Waterloo Bridge. In between that incident and her marriage, she had been in three countries, and starred in two movies, "The Two Headed Spy," filmed on location in West Germany and London, and "The Angry Hills" shot in Greece. She seemed to be racing through life. Even her wedding was hastily prepared. Gia and

Don applied for a marriage license the day before they married in the judge's chambers. Her dress was not new, only the ice sculpture at her reception seemed to be unique.

Don was also on the fast track. He began his acting career about the same time Gia entered Universal International. He started at Columbia Studios; at first he had un-credited roles, not unlike Gia, then worked up to larger parts.

In 1958 MGM contracted Don to co-star in a 26 episodic TV series entitled "Northwest Passage." Don played Ensign Langdon Towne who was portrayed as a Harvard graduate map maker; Don was perfect for the part, photogenic, tall, handsome, and spoke with the kind of authority that comes from a polished education.

Although the series was based upon the era's popular TV Western format, "Northwest Passage" was the story about Major Robert Rogers and his quest to discover a waterway across the United States during the French and Indian wars from 1754 to 1759. The TV drama had gun fights, hostile Native Americans, intrigue, and fine-looking manly protagonists; it co-starred the veteran actor Buddy Ebsen, and the strikingly handsome Keith Larsen. But what distinguished it from other TV Western dramas was the fringed buckskin and it was filmed in color.

After the series ended more opportunities opened up for Don. He was on the path to TV stardom when sadly Rose, his mother, passed away on April 6, 1959, a few months before the marriage. From this Don joined Gia understanding the bereavement one endures from loosing their mother.

My sister depended upon our Mother as her safe harbor in a difficult world. Although Gia was a film star, traveled the world, knew many famous and powerful people, she was relatively naive. Even her close friend William Ramage described her as, "... childlike in some ways ...Gia liked people and trusted them. However, I believe her trust in some instances was misguided."

Gia was 25 years old when she married, physically she was an adult, but there were parts of her personality where emotionally she was more like a 5 or 6 year old child. Her model for marriage and adult behavior was our Mother, who had married a father figure, a man 32 years older than she. Our parents never argued; Mother was not an equal partner in marriage, but more like a child who honored and obeyed a parent.

From this immature paradigm Gia entered into matrimony. Unknowingly, Don became her surrogate parent. While Father was stern and disciplined, Don was Gia's comfort and support zone: The loving, protective father that she had always wanted.

Adding to that misperception, marriage for an Italian Catholic girl meant a life long commitment. It was unperceivable for Gia that marriage could grow and change through time, and even come to an end. She had somewhat of a Pollyanna attitude, perhaps even delusional, but in many ways Gia was not mature.

Don most likely was unaware of the depth of her emotional neediness. On the surface she was a fun loving girl, energetic, and good natured. Adding to that scenario, after he lost his mother, to some degree Gia may have replaced the mother figure for him. That was disastrous because my sister did not possess the emotional maturity to be anyone's mother.

Then there was the situation of the complex pressures of television and movie stardom. She was beautiful, and Don knew what men thought when they saw her. He handsome, charming, gentle, and kind, she understood what drew women to him, and that could create temptations. Stress mounting from emotional levels, their egos on the line, the misconceptions of marriage expectations, it was recognizable that their marriage did not start on firm ground; instead it tittered upon a sharp precipice of ambiguities and misunderstandings.

Gia became what she perceived as the dutiful wife: an excellent cook, an organized homemaker, and a loving individual. She wanted Don to love her so she did what he liked to do. For instance, they enjoyed looking at and discussing art together.

Gia and Don deciding upon what art they should have in their home.

However, Don most likely was unaware of Gia's mindset. For him marriage was a social convention that could provide an acceptable and legal way for a man and a woman to live together, and to have children, but there were also economic opportunities. As Gia's star was rapidly rising and along with it her income, he knew that Gia was not an investment strategist. Money was an important issue. In that area Don mirrored Father who was an astute businessman.

Gia and Don in their backyard on Woodrow Wilson Drive.

While Gia and Don moved through life quickly, nevertheless, they took some time off. The screen writer and movie director Peer Oppenheimer wrote an article for "The Daily Herald," published in the Sunday November 8, 1959, edition. The story featured Don's friend Rock Hudson.

Above: Gia navigating *Good Luck* while the men sleep; Rock to the left of Gia and Don to the right.

It was after Rock filmed "Pillow Talk" with Doris Day, he was becoming a big star, and Oppenheimer thought the readers would want to know what Rock did in between making films. Rock took him out on his 40 foot ketch he called *Khairuzan* –Arabic for *Good Luck*, and invited his friends Don and Gia to come along. It was not mentioned in the article, but Don had taught Rock how to sail during the time they lived at Malibu.

After Don and Gia were married, they bought "his and hers" sail boats. They enjoyed sailing off the Californian coast. Often Rock went along in his ketch. Perhaps Rock felt comfortable and safe sailing alongside his teacher and friend.

Gia, Don, and Rock spent hours together away from Hollywood and the paparazzi on their sail boats far off from the California coast.

Above: Gia on her sailboat.

However, one time when Rock was alone sailing near the coast of Cannes, France, "The Daily News" −of Grand Prairie Texas reported on September 7, 1960, "…he narrowly escaped injury when his boat was rammed…. Eyewitnesses said Hudson dove into the water seconds before the crash. Both boats suffered considerable damage, but no one was injured."

℘

Early in 1960, Gia went unaccompanied to Munich, Germany, to begin filming the story of Dr. Wernher von Braum, the famous missile scientist. The movie "I Aim at the Stars" featured Curt Jürgens as Von Braum. The tall, German built actor had dazzling blue eyes and a shock of flaxen hair. He wasn't exactly handsome, but he was manly and dashing. The type of guy a girl could go to in times of trouble. Jürgens chose Gia to be his female co-star. Fascinated with her looks, he was all a twitter upon meeting her.

She, on the other hand, was in Germany away from her safe harbor, her husband Don. Alone in a country that at one time promoted Nazism and trained Nazi soldiers most likely reminded her of when she lived in the cave in the hills above Mili San Marco during World War II. She needed to feel protected. Where would she turn, or to whom would she turn?

While shooting a movie on location during the 1960's, there were no cell phones where one could call a loved one at any time. Long distance calls were expensive, used for special occasions, and had to be booked ahead of time. Of course, Skype was science fiction.

Being isolated from spouses, families, homes and comfort zones, it is a unique situation somewhat bracketed off from reality. Homesick actors on location unintentionally may misperceive a friendly word from a co-worker. Perhaps overly sensitive to an affable glance from another actor; it is understandable that many times intense relationships develop between actors; a closeness that seems real, conceivably a feeling of falling in love. But when the film wraps, everybody goes their separate ways, the emotions evaporate as they return to everyday life with their familiar surroundings at home.

Gia and Don at home on Woodrow Wilson Drive

Gia was an emotionally needy person, I don't know of the personal relationships that developed while she was filming "I Aim at the Stars," but when she returned home to California, and to Don, one day a gift arrived.

It was a large Beirgarten table, the kind of furniture used during Oktoberfest, and it came with two benches. The benches were so durable that five big men could stand on one.

The present looked expensive, it was unique, and it was from Curt Jürgens. Ordered specially made for my sister, and he had it shipped from Munich. The furniture was large; it needed its own space or room, an extravagant gift, or was it a keepsake, maybe a souvenir of a fond memory? What encouraged Jürgens to be so splendid?

Questions arose that didn't need answers. After 14 months of marriage, Gia and Don went their separate ways.

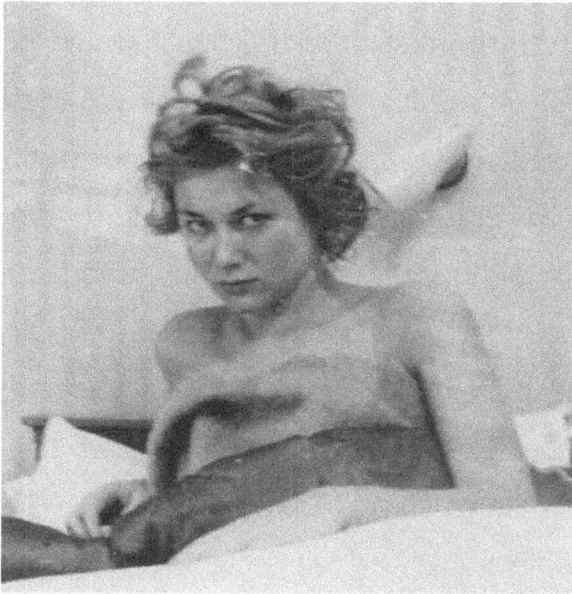

಄

The Guns of Navarone

We were married in August, 1959. Last October we separated for two months before he joined me in London. We've decided not to do that any more –it isn't good." Gia told Hedda Hopper in 1961.

It was the first breakup, but it would not be the last. Their careers stressful and demanding, add to that the anxiety of newly weds being apart for long periods of time. As a result Don wanted Gia to stop making movies, to stay at home and be his wife, although she loved acting, and her career, for the sake of their marriage, she surrendered to his wishes.

There's a Biblical Proverb that's seems apropos at this point, it goes like this, "Man makes a plan, but it is God who determines Man's steps." Don's strategy for Gia to become a stay-at-home housewife went out the window when Gregory Peck agreed to star in "The Guns of Navarone."

Peck, one of the most popular movie stars of the era, was to portray Captain Keith Mallory. His character was a spy who was also a seasoned mountaineer. Eventually he became the leader of the Allied Commando team known as Force 10. That group consisted of the two-time Oscar winner Anthony Quinn, also an Oscar winner David Niven, English actors Stanley Baker, Anthony Quayle, and the teen heartthrob singer / actor James Darren. The team was to rendezvous on Navarone Island with two Partisan resistance fighters who were Maria, played by Irene Papas, and Anna who Gregory Peck insisted my sister be cast in the role.

Although in Alistair MacLean's book the Partisans were portrayed as males; however, the screenwriter and producer Carl Foreman knew that to have a box office successful movie there had to be a love scene; it was part of the film making formula. For that reason Forman reassigned the sex of MacLean's male Partisans to female.

Having women in close contact with a group of virile, strong, and intelligent men created a sexual tension, and a potential opportunity for romance. He chose Peck's character for an indulgence.

But, the love scene wasn't exactly about love; during the team's short stay on Navarone there was no time to build up a proper loving relationship that could be consummated. Raw sex, on the other hand, was not acceptable, unless it was an R-rated film.

Foreman knew that he had to get this right because if it seemed as though Peck's character was taking advantage of the situation, he would loose his command of the moral high ground. If Gia's Anna was too willing, it would have looked as if she joined the Partisan movement to find a man.

To give credibility to her Partisan commitment Forman had her hair cut short and combed back like that of a man, he knew it wouldn't matter if she were bald because Gia was a beautiful woman. He scripted her death scene that she wear a blue gingham dress similar to the one Dorothy wore in "The Wizard of Oz." It seemed to give the character a type of emotional disassociation; what was real? Was it the committed Partisan with a man's haircut or the little girl in a blue gingham dress wanting to go home?

Forman carefully shaped the love scene around the tensions two people shared under the threat of detection by the enemy. If Peck's character was discovered by the Germans, he could have been captured and most likely killed. He knew that if Anna was captured by the Germans that she could be killed, what he didn't know was that she was the German mole.

Because of the multiple conflicting aspects to the love scene, the relationship was doomed. Before Peck's character discovered that Anna was a spy, he was genuinely attracted to her, but he knew when he left the island he'd never see her again. Although she had feelings for Peck's character, she was the only one who knew the underlying truth. Obviously there could be just a single night of passionate dalliance.

The movie was to be shot on the Greek Island of Rhodes. It was a three month location filming schedule, afterwards studio work at Shepperton Studios in England; in total seven months that Gia would be away from Don. He could not join her on the locations because he had obligations to fulfill for the TV shows "Bonanza," "Surfside 6," and "Stagecoach West," all filmed in Los Angeles.

Gia had given her word to Don that she would not make another film on location; to keep that promise was important for her and her marriage. There were other actresses that could play Anna. But, it was Peck who would not accept anyone else but my sister.

I was curious why he insisted upon Gia, and then years later I understood when I saw Peck's wife Veronique Passani. She looked more like Gia's sister than I did. Veronique was a French news reporter who had met Peck in 1952, they married on December 31, 1955, and became inseparable.

Remarkable the physical similarity between my sister and Veronique; the facial bone structure, the eye color, the

European accent, of course Peck wanted Gia to play the part. But, there could be another reason.

When Peck was a young actor and during the filming of Alfred Hitchcock's 1945 film "Spellbound," he had a brief affair with Ingrid Bergman. He admitted to an interviewer that he felt a real love for her. The Hollywood Gossip columnist Erskine Johnson compared my sister to Bergman when he wrote in "The Miami Daily" on Sunday February 27, 1955, that Gia Scala was "the New Ingrid Bergman.... She looks like Bergman and talks like her." There was something that Peck must have perceived that was unique about the chemistry of his character in the movie that only Gia could fulfill.

The money offered to my sister for the film was huge! The most she had ever earned for a picture: $100,000. (In 2015 dollars that would be a little less than $800,000.) From starting out as a contract player at Universal where she made $100 a week, to earning $100,000 dollars co-starring in a major motion picture where she'd share the marquee along with Award winning actors ... it was unbelievable.

With that amount of money Don and Gia could retire for life! Finally it was decided by all parties that Gia would play Anna.

Everyday while away on location Gia wrote to Don. The letters conveyed her feelings and her desires to be with him, *mi tesoro!* -- "My treasure" she called him. (Personally, I believe it was the other way around.) She was devoted to him and she "could never love anyone but" him. However, in between her expressions of amour, she recounted what was happening in her daily life on the set.

There were charming tidbits regarding the actors, one that I recall was about Anthony Quinn, he was a chess aficionado. He had portable chess boards everywhere because between scene set ups he'd play chess. But, then there was his quirky idiosyncrasy: he insisted upon wearing a red tee-shirt under his movie costume. When the outfit got wet -- this happened often -- the undershirt stood out robustly. Peck light-heartedly declared the two-time Oscar winner was a scene stealer. (Peck had not yet won an Academy Award.)

When it came time for the love scene, it was Gia who became the scene stealer. She worked the camera. Even though Peck was one of the most crafted actors in the world, Gia not only seduced Peck's character, but in her close-up she hypnotized the viewer just as Gloria Swanson did when descending the staircase during the final scene of the 1950 film "Sunset Blvd."

As Gia's character submits to Peck's, the closer she leans towards him, the camera moves in, it captures her eyes welling-up; as the tears begin to spill down her cheeks, the question is born? Is she contemplating sensual pleasure, or are her shoes too tight?

I've heard of women crying during sex, but before? Wouldn't that be a turn off? Unless the man was a brute, but Peck's character, although a little shallow, was not a beast. Or perhaps Gia was missing Don. Whatever the reason, the tears do not make sense unless the character she played was thinking about the possible deadly outcome of their liaison.

Later when Gia was discovered as the traitor and her dress was ripped off her back, it was the nudity Foreman needed for the movie, but it didn't create enough surprise to move the film forward.

In MacLean's book Col. Andreas Stavrou, Anthony Quinn's character, was the traitor. Quinn refused to play such a despicable individual. It would have been more shocking if Foreman stayed true to the book.

When Gia character was killed off, there was no surprise, merely movie math for a successful box office film: fight scene plus chase scene add love scene include bad girl gets killed, and so on.

Gia's film criticism was favorable. An example was that of correspondent Shelah Graham. In the "Desert News & Telegram" of Salt Lake City, Utah, she wrote in her August 19, 1961 column:

Gia Scala's career is in high gear since her hit with Gregory Peck in "The Guns of Navarone." She stars with Kirk Douglas in "Two Weeks in Another Town" to be made soon in Italy. Better still — Gia is happy in her marriage to Don Burnett.

There were no negative comments about Gia's participation in the film; but Lynn Hanly in her book "Gregory Peck: a Charmed Life," wrote that Gia Scala was "too pretty" to have played a Partisan.

However, the film's director J. Lee Thompson in May of 2000 reminisced about making "Guns" with Gia. He said that she "was a little crazy ... She was a little upset with me over some scene that we had done ... when she decided I needed a haircut." At that point he began to laugh during the interview with the "Los Angeles Times" reporter Susan King, he continued with "I just sat there while she cut my hair and she ruined it. It made me look ridiculous! I had to wear a hat." But, he reconsidered and said, "In fact, I am not sure that it was a scene from 'Guns' she was upset about. Before 'Guns,' I had done a film with her called 'I Aim at the Stars.' She was absolutely crazy. Although I liked her very much, after the film was finished, I said, 'Thank God. I hope I never have to work with her again.' And then when I inherited 'Guns of Navarone,' who was in the cast? Gia Scala!"

ೞ

The movie's Royal World Wide debut was held on April 27, 1961, in London's Odeon Leicester Square. Afterwards, the cast was presented to Her Majesty Queen Elizabeth II.

ೞ

The film was nominated for an Academy Award in the categories of Best Picture, Best Director, Best Film Editing, Best Sound, Best Original Score, Best writing (adapted screen play). It won the Academy Award for Best Effects, Special Effects.

Above: James Darren, Gia and David Niven.

ೞ

A New Robin in the Hood

G regory Peck earned in the neighborhood of 2 million dollars for "The Guns of Navarone." For those who worked closely with him during the filming, he ordered special gold watches from Cartier. My sister's timepiece was lovely.

The Burnetts together again, this time in London for the film debut; while in Europe, Gia wanted to show-off Don to Father who was living in Sicily.

Gia and Don in Europe

Now that she was rich, had a successful career, and married, she figured Father had to approve of her lifestyle. She may have contemplated that he'd raise objections to Don being an actor, but she was ready to explain her theory of actors should marry actors. She tried it out on Hedda Hopper in an interview for the Chicago Tribune, in 1961. She said,

> I don't see how actors can be married to business people. ...Actors can understand the problems each has to handle. Sometimes you have to study at night for the next day.
> This is a profession that lives on itself; you must talk it out to keep it alive inside yourself. Even if you don't talk much the other actor understands, its empathy. I don't think I could get that response from a banker.

I don't know what went on when Father met Don. For sure he was pleased that she married, but to an actor! Father was a businessman, and an actor a craftsman, they seemed to be miles apart. But beneath the actor façade, Don was a clever businessman. Early on he recognized the amount of money that could be made if one was a successful actor. Once he got into the movie making community, he learned that some stars were terrible managing their money, meaning they squandered it, or they could be talked out of it, or their managers were not trustworthy. Don was uniquely clever with money.

Above: Don and Gia on location for "Il trionfo di Robin Hood." Don is wearing his Robin Hood costume, very short Lederhosen with dark tights / leggings, and boots; he's pointing to a sign that reads "Birotehnik," which is a printing company in Croatia. Gia looks lovely in her "Anna" costume.

Starring in a movie was the way to make big money.
Don had never stared in a picture, but he had the potential.

Critics continually compared him to Rock Hudson, and Rock was making *beaucoup* bucks. While in Europe an opportunity opened up where Don was offered the lead role in an Italian film. He would play Robin Hood and Gia would be his love interest and co-star, not as Maid Marian; strangely her character's name was Anna, like her role in "The Guns of Navarone."

"Now we are working on something in which we'll do a picture together in Italy," Gia recounted to Hedda Hopper. The title of the film was "Il trionfo di Robin Hood" (Robin Hood's Triumph). Parts of the movie such as the Sheriff of Nottingham's castle were filmed in Slovenia.

The Robin Hood film was like a Spaghetti Western where the director was Italian, the cast embraced multi-nationalities and the protagonist was a young and up-coming movie star like Clint Eastwood was in the Sergio Leone's "Man with No Name." This Spaghetti genre pushed Clint Eastwood into stardom, perhaps "Il trionfo di Robin Hood" would be Don's vehicle.

In the scene where Don first appeared he was good-looking, personable, and had somewhat of Errol Flynn's flair. Unfortunately, the director did not provide enough close-ups in order that the audience becomes vulnerable to Don's portrayal of Robin Hood. Instead, the director used shots from the waist up and in natural bright sun light. Don tried not to squint, but his handsome face looked somewhat twisted. The director or editor did not utilize his potential; instead the film was trampled over by the number of horses running through scene after scene. A great deal of the story's momentum was lost with this focus upon the horses, and with the costuming of the Canadian actor and body-builder Samson Burke. He played the part of Little John. His costuming didn't fit the character of Robin Hood's legendary fellow outlaw. Burke wore a short fancy brocade tunic cinched in tightly at the waist with sea-foam blue colored skin-tight tights that showed off every sinewy bulge. Although the costuming didn't work, Burke was a personable actor, great looking body-builder, and there were scenes where he performed acrobatics.

My sister looked beautiful in her first shot, the costume exquisite, she played her part comfortably, and convincingly.

The film debuted in Italy on September 15, 1962, and afterwards made the movie theater circuit in Europe, but not in the United States. Most foreign films with English language subtitles do not do well in US cinemas. However, it played on American television -- a genre where Don was an established actor.

That year Don also made another film in Europe where he co-starred in "Damon and Pythias." He portrayed Pythias to Guy Williams' Damon. Guy a well known actor who played on many television shows during the 1950's and 60's; he was especially remembered as June Lockhart's husband in "Lost in Space." The 6 foot 3 inch tall actor, became an internationally star when Disney cast him as "Zorro."

He began his career as a model in New York. That was when he met Janice Cooper, also a model; they married in 1948.

Guy liked sailing, and owned a 40 foot ketch. Don, Guy and their wives enjoyed sailing together. The two couples became good friends; often spent evenings in one another's company.

⚃

After "Il trionfo di Robin Hood" wrapped up, Don abruptly quit show business. For Gia, the Robin Hood movie was her last for many years. In the fall of 1962, upon returning to California, Don and Gia bought their first home. It was located in an upscale neighborhood in the Hollywood Hills at 7944 Woodrow Wilson Drive. Gia had left her career in films, and moved into her new role as a housewife.

⚃

It's Me, Tina!

Don wanted to become an investment banker; he needed to go to New York for training. Gia went with him. They rented an apartment near Times Square. While there she wanted to introduce her husband to me. At the time I was living in New York because when Dillon and I divorced I didn't know what to do, or where to go. Part of my family was in Ireland, Father was in Sicily, Aunt Agata had become a senior citizen; I was pleased when Aunt Kate invited me to New York.

Gia set up a luncheon date for the three of us in the restaurant at the Algonquin Hotel. It was an elegant setting, with a beautiful atmosphere. When I first saw Don, I remember the uniqueness of his presence. What I mean he was tall and handsome, like many actors, but there was something like a magnetic aura about him. When he entered a room everyone turned to look at him. I recognized that my sister was totally enchanted with her husband. But I was not.

It was not a knee-jerk polarization reaction that happens sometimes between siblings; I looked at him and her with clear eyes.

Gia was in love, or perhaps better said in need. For her Don became everything, she sacrificed her successful acting career to have him. That was a huge! Perhaps she did not take under consideration how fortunate she was to be a movie star. There were millions of girls who would have been overjoyed to have a career such as hers, and would have never given it up. On the other hand, when Don asked her to forgo her career, for me that was not an indication of love; it seemed like a power play. If he loved her, he would want the best for her, and would have helped her to achieve greater success in acting; instead he smashed down her celebrity and her career. For me he was a cool number.

I looked for the glue that kept Gia stuck to him, and decided it was twofold: one was the safe harbor of a loving parent and the other was pure sex. There was this sexual attraction between them that oozed out, and spilled over everywhere. Even though he was good looking, for me he did not have much of a personality; I didn't like him at all.

After Don completed his training, they went back to California. Gia and I continued writing to one another. As time passed, her letters became introspective as she began to complain of how tiresome her days had become since she quit acting. Her life was totally dedicated to helping her husband's new business. She'd hostess business parties in their home where new or potential clients attended. Continually socializing in an effort to promote Don; it sounded like she started to resent him.

While Gia was no longer in show business, I was starting a new career. When I came to New York, I asked myself what should I do to make a living. I enjoyed music; I used to sing when I was a girl. Aunt Kate said I should try my luck at a singing career. When Kate said luck, she meant that I would have a better chance of success if I prepared myself. That I must train with the best voice coach in New York, and that was Carlo Menotti. He had a long list of pupils and former students such as Judy Garland, Harry Belafonte, Tony Bennett and Bobby Darin. When I auditioned for him, he accepted me into his School of Vocal Instructions.

But good singers are more than just a voice; it's how the song is sung, to transmit feelings, and emotions. There are many vocalists, but not all of them express a song in such a way that the listener feels the emotions.

While Maestro Menotti taught me vocal technique, acting school gave me insight to interpreting a song. It was at the Actor's Studio where I began classes. I liked acting,

269

but an actress / singer needs to know how to move in order to convey visually the sentiment. I enrolled in a dance school.

Above: A letter Maestro Menotti wrote for me. As you can see, his signature was exquisite.

Aunt Kate helped me financially with my apartment, but I needed to pay for the classes. I got a modeling job with Loveable Lingerie; I became Miss Loveable Lingerie. I also modeled for McFadden Bartell, and other companies where I appeared in magazines and a few book covers. Luckily a casting director for commercials saw my print work and hired me to do a couple of commercials for television. That was my springboard into TV soaps. I signed with Fifi Oscard's talent agency. She handled models, actors, commercials, and so on.

271

Marie Pigalle Makeup, now known as Pigalle Makeup, used my face in their advertising champagne. I was getting to know many people in New York.

As time passed, I started to date seriously one individual. The journalist Walter Winchell commented in his showbiz column "On Broadway" that appeared on August 6, 1965,

> Actress Tina Scala, a student at the Actor's Studio, will marry Morton Lazarus in September. He owns Calais Originals.

But, the marriage did not come to pass. Instead of becoming a wife, I became the "New York Daily News" Weather Girl.

That job was fun. When the seasons changed, I would be photographed in a seasonal appropriate outfit. Such was the case in the winter of 1966; I was wearing a mini-skirt and boots when the "Daily News" photographer snapped a photo of me making my way over a snow bank in Central Park. That picture went "viral" -- meaning it was so popular that it appeared in most major newspapers across the United States, and some of those papers ended up in military installations.

Soon afterwards, I received fan mail from U.S. soldiers stationed in Vietnam. One letter in particular was from Sgt. Cesar A. Soriano, who served as a spokesman for the mortar platoon of Company D, 2nd Battalion, 1st Infantry, 195th Light Infantry Brigade, serving in Vietnam, he wrote

> about a picture of a young lady by the name of Tina Scala, we have been day after day admiring the picture of the above mentioned brunette. [Tina's photo produced an overpowering urge on behalf of himself and his 43 buddies to correspond with her.] ...Thereby satisfying the many hearts that are throbbing in high gear." *The Muscatine Journal & News.* Monday, February 6, 1967.

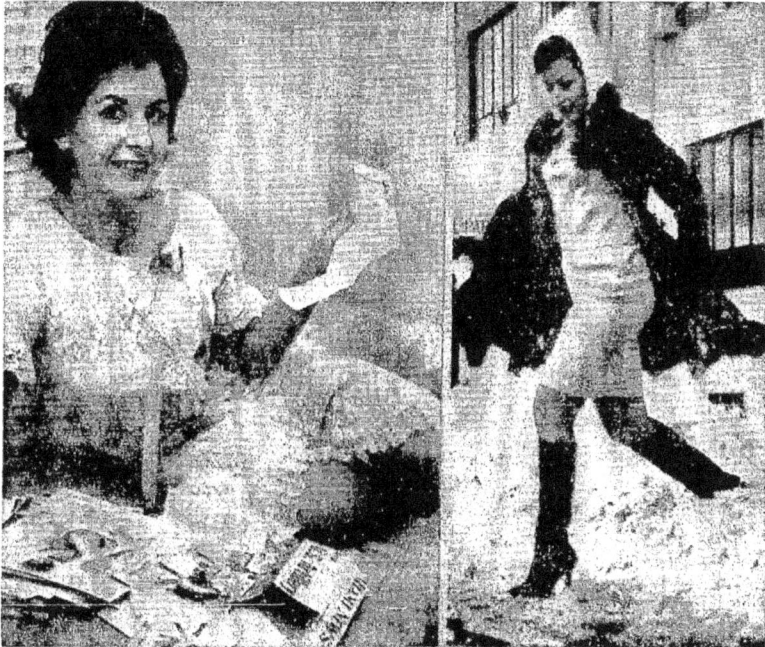

Above: Left, I'm holding one of the many letters I received from service men; Right: the famous photo of me making my way over the snow bank in boots and wearing a miniskirt.

Above: Here I am in my summer attire.

The same year the columnist Earl Wilson wrote in his "Weekend Wrap Up:

> Gia Scala's kid sister Tina makes her film debut with Rock Hudson in "Seconds."
> *Syracuse Herald Journal*, September 25, 1966

I remember when I was on the movie set, I saw Rock, I knew he was friends with my sister, but I was shy, I couldn't go up to him and introduce myself. The movie was a science fiction drama directed by John Frankenheimer.

I liked acting, but those jobs were not as forthcoming as entertaining in night clubs and shows. When I started singing professionally, I heard that Camay Records was having open auditions. Their offices were in the Brill Building that was located at 1721 Broadway in the heart of the theater district. When I went to the office, on display was some of the LPs Camay produced. Artists such as Peggy Lee, Nat "King" Cole,

Lawrence Welk and Frankie Carle, I assumed were under contract with the record label.

Wow! I thought to be among great entertainers like these would be wonderful. After I auditioned, Alan Doyle offered me a contract. I took it home to read it over and to discuss the opportunity with Aunt Kate.

Since I was considering getting seriously into the music business, I thought it was a smart idea to start reading the trade magazine "Billboard." After I had signed with Camay, I discovered an article explaining how Camay got those famous artists on their label.

NEW BUDGET LINE TO BOW: CAMAY LABEL
At press time the trade was buzzing with reports about the debut of a new budget line, Camay Records, whose initial releases would include albums with sides by Capitol artists Nat King Cole, Peggy Lee, and other sides by Lawrence Welk and Frankie Carle. There was considerable speculation as to where the reported Camay masters came from. Camay office stated it would provide more details, but none was forthcoming.
... Tradesters were of the opinion that the Camay master of Cole and Peggy Lee were derived from soundtracks used years ago when Louis Snader produced a series of TV film shorts.

The article was a little misleading because Camay was not a new company; it was founded by Don Ames and Hal Weiss in 1961.

The article continued with,

An interesting aspect of the speculation was the matter of licensing. The Snader licenses were synchronizations rather than mechanicals; and it was questioned whether performances cleared under synchronization license could be transferred to disk without authorization.
Billboard, May 30, 1964.

Camay had produced a few 45's, but not until the Snader Telescriptions -- also known as visual records for TV -- did the label come out with a LP. Camay stripped out the sound tracks from the Telescriptions and then waxed them into LPs.

Louis D. Snader was the man behind the concept of Telescriptions. He had been a musician, and was a real estate tycoon who owned a number of movie theaters in Southern California. He became an independent television producer and in 1950 produced the television shown "Dick Tracy;" later, after he named himself the executive producer of his company, Snader hired "Duke" Goldstone as director, editor, and producer of the pre-syndicated 1952 version of "The Liberace Show."

In 1949 Snader wanted to make his mark in television with Telescriptions. These were 3 minute filmed musical performance that featured famous singers like Peggy Lee, Nat "King" Cole, and others. Filming twelve Telescriptions a day at a cost of $2,500 each, after two years he had a catalogue of about 360 Telescriptions; his plan was to lease them cheaply to local TV stations as fillers for their daily TV programming. The TV stations were appreciative because to produce and to film programs was expensive. Snader also wanted to use them in a TV program that would be hosted by TV disc jockeys – he was attempting to mimic radio's DJs for television. When the plan didn't work out, Snader's partners in the business decided to sell the catalogue. Studio Films purchased it for $600,000.

Of course I did not know that Camay Records produced very few records, and that they leased songs from other concerns, and I had no idea about the Telescriptions. Camay's entire catalog of 44 LPs was issued in one year, and that was 1963.

I began to question why Camay gave me a contract. But, I was not the only one with whom they contracted; they held many auditions and were actively seeking new talent. Looking back, I suppose Camay was betting on their new talent that some would make it big, and Camay would reap big bucks selling the contracts. Camay seemed to disappear some time in 1965.

ॐ

In show business there are many independent producers, sometimes these guys are not really producers but say they are and hold auditions just to meet girls. They have no intention of producing anything other than a good time.

I had run into a couple of these situations. It was bothersome and annoying that I wasted my time and energy to go to the audition. But, some guys will try almost anything to get a date. Even though there were some bad apples in the big apple, the majority of my experiences in New York City were positive.

My Aunts Julia and Kate were supportive concerning my new career. Both of my aunts came to New York as young women. Kate arrived in 1927. She worked as a nurse in the Hospital for Joint Disease. A year later her sister Joan –known as Hannah when a child -- joined her; and also worked as a nurse in the same hospital, they shared an apartment in Manhattan. But Joan returned to Ireland in 1954.

On the other hand, Aunt Julia was twelve years younger than Kate. She arrived to New York much later. She worked as a dressmaker, and lived in the city, but after she married, she moved with her husband to Bethel, Connecticut, and continued to live there after her husband died.

My Aunts Julia and Kate were very different from each other. Kate never married, but she was beautiful with blue eyes, and dark blond hair. She was neat, gentle, reserved, and somewhat formal. However, Julia was Black Irish; she had a wildly kept shock of dark raven colored hair, with eyes the color of a Robin's egg. She was spontaneous, frank and somewhat of a hillbilly.

I used to visit Julia in Bethel on weekends. She lived on an enormous estate that had a great deal of land; better described as a mansion with a forest around it, where wild animals roamed about. Often she'd let hunters onto her land. I remember one time; I was there when some hunters came to the house to ask Aunt Julia permission to hunt on her land. I stepped outside away from the house somewhat, the hunters were talking to me. All of a sudden, I heard a loud blast; I turned to where the noise came from and saw Aunt Julia with a huge shotgun. She had let off a shot above their heads, but then she pointed the gun towards the men and yelled out, "Leave my niece alone; you came to hunt, so hunt, or else get out of here!"

Aunt Julia liked to take a nip; it was rum punch that was her drink. I'd sit with her in the grand dining room where there was a beautiful table and candelabra that once was owned by the German Kaiser William II. After a drink or two she'd start singing "Smoke Gets in Your Eyes." Aunt Julia didn't like to drink alone, so she'd pour me one. When she was in her cups, I'd go to the bathroom and pour out my drink. But, she'd pour me another, and another.

She owned lovely things, I remember one in particular, a piece of jewelry; it was a heart shaped diamond that was the center piece of a diamond necklace. That stone must have been about ten karats in size. She kept it in her tall, heavy metal floor safe, an old fashioned one like the banks used. One day, when she went to town, some thieves broke into her home. They knew about the diamond, and tried to open the safe. They couldn't so they blew up the safe and stole the diamond necklace. They broke up the large diamond, and took the other stones out of the necklace; then tried to sell them. The police caught the thieves.

Often Aunt Julia went to New York to have lunch with Kate and me. We would go to the most exclusive restaurant in the city. After a big fabulous lunch, Aunt Julia always asked the waiter for a doggie bag. Kate became embarrassed. How could she ask for a doggie bag in a first class restaurant? Kate tired to mitigate her sister's behavior, and told the waiter as an excuse that her sister had a large dog. Julia snapped back with, "That's not true! I'm going to eat it myself after I get home."

There seemed to be a kind of sibling rivalry between the two Aunts. While Kate comported herself very much like a lady, lived in a Manhattan apartment with a view of Central Park, had an income and a few investments; but she did not have an equal level of financial security like her little sister. Julia had married a rich man who had owned a seat on the Stock Exchange. From him she learned investing, and acquired a good sum of money when he passed away.

Kate the proper Aunt often treated me to lunch at her favorite restaurant. Wearing a beautiful suit, with a smart hat, gloves, and matching handbag, she'd wait till the waiter offered her a chair, and then sat down at the table. Everyone knew her at that restaurant. The waiter greeted her and then asked if it were her birthday. "Why, yes!" she said, "You remembered." With that he brought a complimentary celebratory drink, and then another, and another. This went on every time we went to her favorite restaurant, and we ate there often. One time in particular, after lunch, I said to Aunt Kate, "Let's go to my apartment and call Gia."

"Wonderful! Good idea," Kate said.

She sat on my davenport prim and proper, never crossing her legs, keeping her knees demurely together, her purse resting upon the coffee table, and her gloved hands folded on her lap. Her little white hat perfectly perched upon her head, and her hair flawlessly quaffed.

I reached for the telephone and dialed Gia's number in California. When she answered, I said, "It's me, Tina! I'm here with our Aunt Kate; I'll pass the phone to her." At that moment, as Aunt Kate reached for the telephone she took a nosedive onto the floor; a result of having one too many celebratory drinks.

I took the phone from Kate's hand and said, "Gia …Aunt Kate can't talk right now. I'll call you later. Ciao."

ଔ

Rear Ended!

While I lived in New York I worked a great deal. One of my memorable experiences was the part I played in the 1969 film "Midnight Cowboy." The costume department gave me black wig and stuffed my middle with a pillow; I portrayed a young pregnant woman in a Laundromat. Dustin Hoffman's Ratso was a clever hustler who was continually broke. In our scene he had washed his clothes, but didn't have enough money for the dryer. As I was putting my clothes into the dryer he said "here let me help you." and quickly added his clothes to mine.

I liked Dustin, he was kind, and we laughed a lot. But his co-star Jon Voight − who played Joe Buck a want-a-be gigolo —was never out of character. He flirted.

New York was a good place to work and to live; I have fond memories. The people friendly, the restaurants fabulous, and I enjoyed visiting with my Aunts. However, things began to change when Aunt Julia suffered a stroke. I visited her in the hospital, but she did not recognize me. A few days later, she passed away.

Aunt Kate was nearing her eightieth-first birthday. She remembered her mother, my grandmother, lived a long life, until she was eighty-nine. Kate didn't want to spend the rest of her life away from Ireland, and the family farm. After she left New York, I was alone without family. New York winters at times were brutally cold. I thought perhaps it was time to be near Gia in California, and to live in a warmer climate.

While my sister no longer made movies, she took some acting jobs on televisions shows. At that time for a movie actress to appear in TV shows, it was considered, among some in the business, a downgrade. But, she kept busy while Don was employed with the investment banking firm of White, Weld & Co.

Gia and Don compromised; she worked, but not in movies and not away from Hollywood. Even though she gave up a film career to be Don's wife, homemaker, and cook, it wasn't enough. He complained that Gia did not become pregnant. That it was her fault there were no children. When Gia was in Italy, she had gone to our cousin who was a gynecologist, after he examined her; he said that she was fine, and could have children. Perhaps Don used that issue as a pretext to get out of their marriage. Whatever the reason, he left her for good in March of 1969.

She didn't know where he went, or where he was living, but she had heard gossip that he moved in with Rock Hudson. Late one night she drove to Rock's house to see if it was true. When she found Don's 1957 Cadillac Coupe Deville convertible in Rock's driveway, she became angry, then furious. In a red hot moment she drove her car into the rear end of Don's Caddy. She backed her car out then drove it again smashing the rear of his car, and then again. When Don heard the noise, he looked out the window, and saw her. He called the police. She drove off. The next day, Don sent Gia a bill for the damage.

She told me she enjoyed rear ending his car; I couldn't blame her for being human, letting her emotions take over. She loved him, she devoted herself to him; after he left, she was shattered. That was when her life started to fall apart.

ଔ

Alone

Gia alone at "Raintree County "preview, Lowe's Theater, Times Square.

> Former actress Gia Scala, 33, has sued her husband of 10 years, former TV actor Donald James Burnett, 38, for divorce in Los Angeles. Miss Scala and Burnett, now a stockbroker, have no children.
> *Milwaukee Journal*, March 14, 1969, pg 2.

When Gia filed for divorce on March 13, 1969, it became gossipy news for the media. Even though my sister was appearing as an actress on popular TV shows, she was reported as a former actress. That must have been disheartening to be considered a "has been actress;" and from the newspaper reports she was also a "has been wife." She was no longer the young film ingénue, instead approaching 40; emotionally it was a difficult time for her.

She wanted Don back, but by the fall of 1969, when Don did not come home, Gia decided to go to Europe. She leased her house to Sally Kellerman; it was just about the time that Sally auditioned for the part of Major Margaret "Hot Lips" Houlihan in Robert Altman's movie *MASH*. She loved the house and was pleased that Gia lent it to her.

While in Pairs, Gia studied cooking at the Cordon Bleu. Her motivation was to become a better cook, in order to entice her husband to return. She also studied fine-art painting. Because Don was a landscape painter, she thought if she bettered her skills in art her husband might become interested in her. For me it was delusional thinking. But, she believed she could get him to return home with her cooking and her art.

While in Paris, Gia lived in her friend Henry Miller's apartment. Meanwhile he resided in Pacific Palisades, California. Although married to Hoki Tokuda, who was a concert pianist; Henry most of the time was alone because his wife was on tour or in her native Japan.

Miller wrote to Hoki daily expressing his love, admiration, and obsession for her, but as a free spirit he admitted "I have love affairs and passing fancies...but only from desperation." Hoki didn't even open his letters.

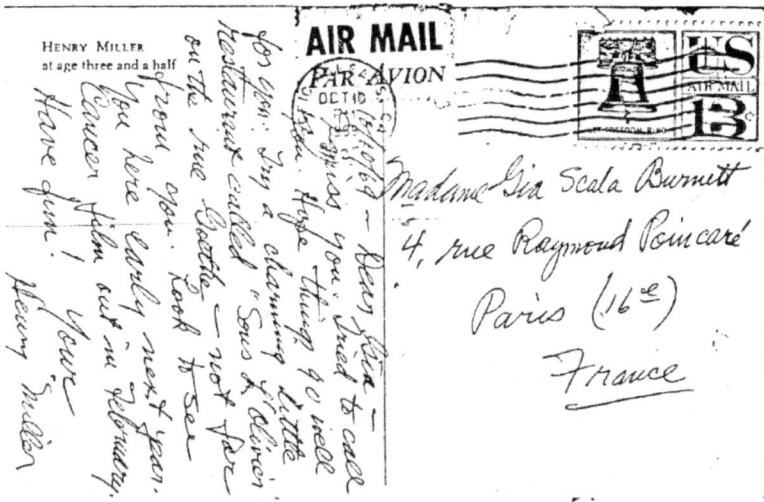

Above: Postcard from Henry Miller to Gia, October 1969.

Hoki Japanese, English her second language, she had commented that she couldn't read through her husband's novels. Although Miller's first published book "Tropic of Cancer" was received well in Europe, it was banned in the United States on the grounds it was pornographic. But in 1964, the US Supreme Court ruled the novel was not obscene, instead it was literature. The outcome of this case was one of the notable events that have become known as the sexual revolution.

In his novels Miller wrote graphically of sexual encounters, not love. Perhaps his unrequited love for his wife created questions that opened up mazes where he stumbled through theorizing why women were the way they were. Drawn to female theatrical types, among his labyrinths were Geraldine Fitzgerald Hildegard Knef, Ziva Rodann, Ava Gardner, Kim Novak, Diane Baker, Inger Stevens, and my sister. Henry wrote candidly to his wife. In his May 14, 1968, letter he reported:

> Tomorrow I'll have champagne lunch with Gia Scala who kept me on the phone three-quarters of an hour (midnight) last night telling me the story of her life.

In a 2011 interview with "Los Angeles Times" reporter John M. Glionna, Hoki explained that during her 11 years married to Miller the relationship was never consummated,

> I kissed Henry just once and he was a terrible kisser. ...It was not romantic ...it was wet.

At one time the actress Christa Lang, and her husband Samuel Fuller, screen writer, novelist, and film director, lived down the street from my sister. When Gia invited Henry to her home for lunch, she asked Christa and Samuel to join them. The couple hit it off with Henry, especially Christa. They became friends and wrote to each other a great deal especially during the time Samuel was in Europe shooting the films "Dead Pigeon," and "Riata."

By 1970 when I relocated to Los Angeles, Gia and Don were still married, but not living together. I took an apartment on Sunset Blvd. not far from her home on Woodrow Wilson Drive. I felt she needed her privacy, and so did I. But we visited.

She'd invite me for lunch at her home. Gia was a fabulous cook. She'd whip up a delicious meal, after she drank a couple of glasses of wine, she'd talk about Don. Even though he was gone, and she had filed for divorce, she'd write love poems to him. She could not give up on the marriage. Lonely and missing him, when she read me the poems out loud, it was pitiful. Continually, perhaps better said obsessively -- she talked about him. They had separated and reconciled a couple of times before she filed for divorce. For her he was on hiatus, she believed that Don would return.

Above R. to L: Gia, Christa Lang, and Henry Miller. This photograph was taken in Henry's Pacific Palisades home.

In the meantime Gia adopted a dog. When I came to visit her new friend, she called out to her pet "Come here Dillon!"

Surprised at the name she gave him, I asked "Why Dillon?" Even more outrageous was her answer:

"I couldn't name him Don because when Don comes home, there would be two Dons in the house. So, I named him Dillon ... after all, look at him. Doesn't he remind you of someone?"

Above: Dillon and Gia

I stayed over that night. Dillon slept on the floor between the two beds. When he started snoring loudly, Gia and I laughed so much. I thought I was going to pee.... I got it why she named him Dillon. She had a "charming" wit.

Almost a year and a half after she filed for divorce, the case was heard on September 1, 1970 before the Honorable Judge Everett M. Porter of the Superior Court of California, Los Angeles County. The Interlocutory Judgment of Dissolution of Marriage was entered in the Judgment Book on September 29, 1970.

California attempts to avoid divorce; the Interlocutory Judgment is not a final decree; instead it is a six month cooling off period for the parties to reconsider divorce. During that time the couple continues to be married. If one should die, the other can inherit their spouse's estate.

However, Gia and Don did not stipulated to that issue in the Interlocutory; most likely because neither one was contemplating death. But, after the interlocutory time elapsed, a decree of divorce must be filed with the court in order for the divorce to become final.

The six month waiting period was a little confusing. The case was heard on September 1, 1970. When Gia discovered that Don married the actress Barbara Anderson on February 14, 1971, she was devastated. She cried, and cried, but then she counted the days from the Interlocutory decree to his wedding date. It was 16 days short of the six month cooling off period; therefore, Don was still legally married to Gia when he wed Barbara. My sister laughed when she thought about her husband being married to two women at the same time, and his new role as a bigamist. Now she had him!

But, later when she discovered that the Interlocutory time started on the date the court acquired jurisdiction of the respondent (Don), meaning when he was served the Summon, that date was March 13, 1969. By the time Don married Barbara, the Interlocutory time period had been met. When

Gia found out she lost Don, that they were in fact divorced, she seemed to have lost her mind.

She discovered that detail about the Interlocutory timing when we were at the 1971 Pebble Beach Celebrity Tennis Tournament. It was during the July 4th weekend Clint Eastwood held his annual event at the Del Monte Estates. He'd invite a passel of celebrities hoping to attract donations for his charity, and publicity for the stars.

Maggie, Clint's wife, was a good tennis player; when Gia lived at the Villa Sands Apartments she got to know her. She invited my sister to the affair, and Gia asked me to accompany her.

We arrived at Pebble Beach, but the hotel was booked up. The hotel management made some phone calls; they arranged that we could stay in the home of "The King of Lettuce." In Europe when one stays with a King, it was a humongous prestige. I thought Wow! I've never stayed in a King's palace. But, how can there be a Kingdom in a democratic country. Then I discovered that it was a nickname because he was the largest lettuce grower in the area. His name was Mr. Neil.

During the early evening after the tournament concluded there was a big and fancy cocktail party held for all of the celebrities. That was the first time I met Clint. Oh, he was impressive, tall, very tall, and nice; he was an utterly elegant man, and quite handsome.

Everybody was there, I remember meeting Merv Griffin: a lovely man, with a wonderful speaking voice. I was talking with James Garner and his wife Lois when suddenly I felt something similar to a déjà vu. I looked around for Gia, she was not there. I walked out onto the grounds, and then I saw her running towards the cliffs. She had on a white dress, I knew it was her. I screamed for help. Two busboys heard me and saw what was going on. They grabbed her just as she was going to jump off the cliff.

Someone at the party must have cleared up the issue concerning her divorce, which gave her reason to drink, and she became drunk, she didn't know what she was doing. That was the second time I saved her life.

The story of Gia running towards the cliffs was reported in the local newspaper by a well-known writer who attended the cocktail party.

Name, Address and Telephone Number of Attorney(s):

DENTZEL, SMITH & DOCTROW
Attorneys at Law
14540 Haynes Street, Suite 100
Van Nuys, California 91411

785-9610 -- 873-1353

Attorney(s) for.... the respondent

Space Below for Use of Court Clerk Only

ENTERED IN JUDGMENT BOOK NO. 6576,
PAGE 317, on Sept. 29, 1970.

SUPERIOR COURT OF CALIFORNIA, COUNTY OF LOS ANGELES

In re the marriage of

Petitioner: GIA SCALA BURNETT

and

Respondent: DONALD JAMES BURNETT

CASE NUMBER

D 744 737

INTERLOCUTORY JUDGMENT OF
DISSOLUTION OF MARRIAGE

This proceeding was heard on ..Sept. 1, 1970.. before the Honorable ..EVERETT M. PORTER,.
Judge Pro Tem, sitting as such by order of the presiding Judge and pursuant to written
Department No....2-B ..... stipulation of the parties

The court acquired jurisdiction of the respondent on ..March 13, 1962.. by:
(Date)

☐ Service of process on that date, respondent not having appeared within the time permitted by law.

☒ Service of process on that date and respondent having appeared.

☐ Respondent on that date having appeared.

The court orders that an interlocutory judgment be entered declaring that the parties are entitled to have their marriage dissolved. This interlocutory judgment does not constitute a final dissolution of marriage and the parties are still married and will be, and neither party may remarry, until a final judgment of dissolution is entered.

The court also orders that, unless both parties file their consent to a dismissal of this proceeding, a final judgment of dissolution be entered upon proper application of either party or on the court's own motion after the expiration of at least six months from the date the court acquired jurisdiction of the respondent. The final judgment shall include such other and further relief as may be necessary to a complete disposition of this proceeding, but entry of the final judgment shall not deprive this court of its jurisdiction over any matter expressly reserved to it in this or the final judgment until a final disposition is made of each such matter.

Pursuant to the stipulation in open Court by and between the parties, with the approval of their respective attorneys, the Court makes the following additional orders:

1. COMMUNITY PROPERTY. The community property of the parties is awarded as follows:

a. The parties' family home, commonly known as 7344 Woodrow Wilson Drive, Los Angeles, California 90046, and legally described as:

Dated...

....
Judge of the Superior Court

Form Adopted by Rule 1287 of
Judicial Council of California
Effective January 1, 1970

INTERLOCUTORY JUDGMENT OF
DISSOLUTION OF MARRIAGE

1287

Gia... Not Herself

Gia's personality changed after Don left in 1969. She became an unhappy, contentious and bitter individual. I remember one time she invited me to lunch at the Brown

Derby. She ordered steak tartar, when the waiter brought her the meal; she tasted it and immediately told the waiter to "take it away." Making a disgusted expression, she said it was terrible. When the waiter opened the bottle of expensive wine that she asked for, he poured a little of the wine in her glass, she tried it, and told him "That's awful, take it away." She got up to leave and I followed.

A few weeks later, she invited me to eat with her at a swanky restaurant in Beverly Hill. We had just sat down at the table, when she saw two producers. She turned to me and said, "Let's go. I don't want to see them and I especially don't want them to see you."

Beyond our private relationship, publicly Gia was becoming a menace. She had too much to drink one night and had driven her car fast on twisty Mulholland Drive; when she lost control of the car, it went off a cliff, rolled over several times down the hill, and came to a stop upside down. The emergency ambulance crew and the police when they saw the accident at first thought there was a death. She was taken to the emergency room; she had some bruises, minor lacerations and lost the tip of her right index finger. It was incredible that she was not killed. But she was sited for drunk driving.

On another occasion I received a phone call from her. She was at Sybil Brand Institution arrested for drunk driving. I went there to bail her out.

Then she was arrested for disturbing the peace. She and an acquaintance Allen S. Bershin, who was a 22 years old busboy, had gotten into a fight with the parking lot attendant where she had parked her rented car. It was in The Pantry Restaurant's lot in downtown Los Angeles. Both were booked on suspicion of battery, which was a felony! The incident appeared in many newspapers throughout the United States:

> Municipal Judge Irwin J. McBroom imposed sentence after Miss Scala pleaded no contest to a misdemeanor charge of disturbing the peace in a dispute over a 50-cent fee. When the judge told her a condition of probation was that she not associate with known narcotic users, Miss Scala objected, saying, "I have never been around such people." The judge said the condition is standard in probation cases.
> *The Daily Mail* from Hagerstown, Maryland, July 28, 1971, pg. 15.

The parking lot attendant, Serhad Naderi, reported to the police that he was pummelled by both the actress and her companion. However, the judge mitigated the battery charge to a misdemeanour "with strings." Gia was placed under two years of probation and fined $125; Bershin was given three years probation and also fined $125.

During this time in Gia's life, I was dating a medical doctor. Occasionally I made us dinner at my apartment. We were about to begin to eat when the phone rang. It was from the hospital. Gia was in the emergency room. I asked my boyfriend to accompany me, he did, and when we arrived at the hospital, he consulted with the doctor about her condition. Afterwards, he told me that Gia had ingested the drug Ketamine; medically employed as a sedative and anesthesia. But when used recreationally it produced dissociate states characterized by a sense of detachment from one's body and the physical world. She took enough of the drug to kill a couple of horses. He said it was a miracle she survived. The hospital reported the incident as a drug overdose.

California considered that type of behavior as an endangerment to one's self and perhaps to others. For that reason Gia was taken to the Ventura County Hospital and put under psychiatric observation for seventy-two hours. Afterwards she was committed, but she wanted out.

Without my knowledge, Anna Kashfi, the actress whom Gia replaced in the 1957 film "Don't Go Near the Water," agreed to take care of my sister. She told the court that Gia would live with her and her son, and that she was able to care for Gia round the clock because she was not working. She asked the court to have Gia released under her care. I

300

couldn't believe that the court and the hospital agreed to Anna's request, nevertheless, Gia went to live with her.

When she left the hospital, she did not tell me. Only later she called to say that she was staying with Anna and her thirteen year old son Christian, who was born during Anna's marriage to Marlon Brando.

In Darwin Porter's book, "Brando Unzipped," he wrote that at the time Brando married Anna Kashfi "he was secretly dating her friend Gia Scala." I found that difficult if not impossible to believe. Brando and Anna married in 1957, that year Gia was very busy. She worked in four films, and was consumed with worry over the health of our Mother.

Gia had met Brando when she was a contract player at Universal. He had given informal talks to the new actors and actresses that the studio hired. There was never an affair with Brando, I would have found out. Besides, Brando was not her type, he was too short.

Anna and Brando divorced in 1959; it was a contentious divorce, there were vicious fights over the custody of Christian. Marlon refused to give Anna money for their son's maintenance. She had worked in a few films, but not enough to support herself and her son. She had to find other ways to make money. I believe she took care of my sister because Gia paid her. Later I found canceled checks where my sister did give her money.

After two months of living with Anna, Gia called to ask if I would pick her up. She gave me the address and the time. Anna lived in Boyle Heights, an area located to the east of downtown Los Angeles; it was a working class neighborhood where the average yearly income was the lowest in the city.

They were living in a bungalow that had a patio area in the front. I arrived early and sat down on one of the patio chairs. I remember the place was messy, and trashy. Awhile later Anna's boyfriend arrived. I didn't know him. He sat down, some time passed before we started conversing. About two hours later Gia, Anna, and Christian drove up. When Anna got out of the car, she gave me a dirty look. Gia invited me inside where I saw beer bottles, trash, dirty dishes in the sink, it was just awful. After I took Gia home, I got a phone call from Anna. She started screaming at me that I was flirting with her boyfriend that she was going to beat me up. She talked crazy on the phone. I hung up.

My sister didn't look good after the two months she supposedly recuperated at Anna's. To feel better about herself, Gia wanted to buy a few new pieces of clothing. She told me that she had admired my style and asked if I would help her pick out some things. But, she wasn't feeling well enough to go shopping. I decided to give her some of my clothes which she said she had liked. Later on, I was disappointed when I learned that she gave away the clothes I had given her. It just didn't make sense, like so many other things she did such as living with Anna in that miserable dump, getting drunk, driving her car off a cliff, fighting with a parking-lot attendant over 50-cents. She wasn't thinking correctly, she was not herself.

Then Daniel La Biena entered my sister's life. He had worked as a handyman for one Gia's neighbors. She wanted to make some repairs on her home so she offered to let him live in the room above her garage in exchange for the work.

But, here was where the story gets weird. After La Biena settled in, he invited three of his buddies to move into Gia's house!

It didn't look right. But, what could I do?

ঙ

Sadly a Short Life

The night before Gia died, Jan and Guy Williams picked up my sister from her home to take her to dinner. Upon returning, while driving up the street towards the house, they could see that someone was peeking out of one of the windows. Gia said it was her handyman Daniel La Biena. She commented that she invited him to live in the room above the garage in exchange for work on her home. After he settled in, and when one day she was away, he had three of his friends move into her house. She objected and asked them to leave, but they would not. She told Jan and Guy that she was going to have all of them forcibly evicted as soon as possible.

On April 30, 1972; the day of her death, she called the Police in the morning. They arrived and told the four men to leave; which they did.

But, La Biena returned. He called the Police around six in the evening, however, that didn't mean he arrived at her home at that time. When the Police got there, he told them he found Gia's front door wide open, she was lying on top of her bed nude, when he went to wake her, she was unresponsive and cold to the touch.

The Police saw that next to her bed were empty wine bottles, dirty glasses, and a vial that contained her prescription for Valiums. Because a few months earlier when Gia had taken the Ketamine, the media mistakenly reported that she attempted to take her life. From that antecedent, the Police concluded her death was a suicide.

After the autopsy, Gia's cause of death was changed to accidental intoxication of ethanol and barbiturates. There were three Valiums tablets missing from her prescription. When were the Valiums taken? It could have been anytime, perhaps weeks before she died. Or someone else could have taken the pills out of the bottle. But Valium was not a barbiturate, it's a benzodiazepine. Contrary to what was found next to her bed-- Valium, and what was found in her body - barbiturates –I became suspicious.

Thomas Noguchi often referred to as the "coroner to the stars," was a meticulous Medical Examiner. He had determined the cause of death of many high profile cases such as that of Marilyn Monroe.

He recorded Marilyn's cause of death was due from acute barbiturate poisoning. He specified Choral Hydrate and

Nembutal found in her body. Likewise, barbiturates, not Valium was found in my sister's body. My big question was who provided the drugs that killed my sister?

In 1972, the law in California was vague about the liability of drug dealers; mostly I presume because big pharmaceutical companies were also a kind of drug dealer. It wasn't until the actor Carroll O'Connor lost his son, Hugh, in 1995, to a cocaine addiction. The facilitator was a street drug dealer. When O'Connor brought evidence to the Police that the person who furnished the drugs for his son's addiction had a causal connection to his son's death, that individual was arrested and later convicted. He spent a year in jail, fined $1,000, and ordered to 200 hours of community service.

Later O'Connor persuaded the California legislature to enact a law that made drug dealers liable for the harm they cause to their victims. Presently there are seventeen states in the Union that have passed the Model Drug Dealer Liability Act.

I agree that my sister died from a drug overdose, but again, who provided the barbiturates that killed her? The stigma attached to drugs often blinds people to other perspectives. But, in Gia's case, certain circumstances were overlooked. After her death, there were other peculiarities.

When the newspapers reported her death, unfortunately they gave her home address. This could have alerted potential thieves or souvenir hunters of an opportunity. But, the media did not report who else lived in her home, or if she lived alone. There was not much time that lapsed between the newspaper report and when her house was broken into. Unless thieves had been casing her house for a period of time, only someone with close and personal knowledge knew the real circumstances.

When I discovered that large pieces of her furniture had been removed from the home, I knew that was not an easy task. There had to have been moving trucks that pulled up in front of her house. Several strong men were needed for the job; they had to have used hand-dollies, ropes, furniture skins and other mover's tools. There was movement coming and going, the task was not a quite one, nor one that would be unnoticed in her affluent and tranquil neighborhood.

After I discovered the theft, I asked the neighbors if they had seen anything like moving trucks in front of Gia's house. It was "no," hadn't seen a thing. From my questions I saw expressions of apathy and disapproval in their faces. For them what would they have gained by calling the Police? Later to become a witness in a criminal trial; the neighbors did not want to get involved.

I thought it was peculiar that La Biena returned to Gia's house on the day that he was kicked-out. My sister most likely was still stinging from the terrible situation that he created. If she saw him, it would have upset her. Following her death, I found a note that he had written to her,

Dear Gia —
It is not a matter of understanding one another; it is a matter of understanding one.
Daniel, '72

I thought that note was somewhat unclear, perhaps he was attempting to paraphrase the ancient Chinese philosopher and poet Lao Tzu, who wrote:

He who knows others is wise; he who knows himself is enlightened.

"Dear Gia" La Biena penned, it sounded as if he knew her on a personal level. What kind of handyman was he? I knew she was lonely, she needed a man, and she wanted to be loved; I asked myself had La Biena manipulated himself into her boudoir through Taoism?

Who was this guy?

When he found her dead, fearful, perhaps, that someone saw him at her home even though he was evicted earlier that day. To deflect suspicion, coolly he called the Police. When they questioned him, he said he returned to thank Gia for letting him live there. For the Police, that answer was OK.

However, for me it didn't make sense. Why didn't he telephone her before he arrived? I'm sure she would have told him to get lost. Instead without notice he appeared at her house. If he wanted to thank her, why not do it the next day, why the same day he was evicted?

As I mentioned before, on Gia's phone bill I found a call was made from her telephone after midnight on May 1, 1972, the day after she died.

Who made that call? ... And why?

Above: The Amended Death Certificate

෯

The Funeral

As I watched the pallbearers lift my sister's coffin from the gurney, I felt a merciful dullness come over me. Numb from the heartbreaking reality that it was Gia's casket, but I knew when the dullness faded, for the rest of my life I would feel the pain of her death. While I had survived the loss of our Mother, Grandmother, Aunt Agata, Aunt Julia, and Father, they were of another generation. I missed them terribly, but with my sister's death I felt as if half of me died and was in the coffin that the pallbearers were lifting from the gurney.

I watched the faces of the men who were part of the ancient ritual of carrying the casket. There was Guy Williams, known throughout the world as Zorro. When Gia and I were girls, if someone would have told us that Zorro would be a pallbearer at Gia's funeral, we would most certainly have laughed because it was absurd, just beyond belief. Then again, if someone told us that my sister would become an internationally famous movie actress, a lovely thought, but the odds for that happening would be a million to zero. But, here we are, Zorro, the pallbearer, Gia the international movie actress, and me.

Next to Guy stood Terry Kingsley, he was a beloved actor and screenwriter. He had penned several screenplays for the popular television show "Daniel Boone." Following in his mother's footsteps as a scriptwriter, he was the son of the prolific screenwriter Dorothy Kingsley. She had written "Don't Go Near the Water," Gia's first starring film. I watched his youthful face that was serious and pale as his white gloved hand held one of the thick metal casket handles, he did not look up from his task.

As I looked at each of the six men, I stopped abruptly at the last; a cold shiver went down my spine that worked its way out of my body into my fingertips. I was looking at Don Burnett.

At one time he loved Gia, but she didn't love him, she adored him, worshiped him, he was her *tesoro* "her treasure." Until the day she died she waited for him to return to her. He knew it, but what went on between them cannot be wiped away. Although I did not care for Don when I met him that did not mean he wasn't a classy guy. It must have been difficult for him to be one of the pallbearers that carried his ex-wife's casket to her grave.

C3

The day before the funeral Dore Freeman helped me to make the arrangements. We had gone to Westview Memorial Chapel in Culver City. I selected a bronze coffin with a bas-relief of the Last Supper on the lid. Dore gently said to me, "You don't have to choose the most expensive one."

I replied, "Gia deserves the best."

I had brought with me her burial clothes. From Gia's closet I selected a beautiful Donald Brooks gown, silvery with a purple turtleneck. I also brought the amethyst ring that I had given her on her thirty-eighth birthday only six weeks earlier. I wanted her to be buried with it.

Afterwards Dore took me back to my apartment to rest before the Rosary that evening. Everything was moving so fast. I couldn't believe that a few days earlier I was at the morgue; I was there to identify her. I didn't see Gia's body; instead the L.A. coroner was compassionate, I saw a slide picture that was projected onto a screen. She looked like she just got out of her swimming pool, her hair soaking wet and stringy. There was no doubt it was Gia.

The identification was a formality because I had already read of her death that morning in the "Los Angeles Times." It was on page three of the main news section:

> Found dead – actress Gia Scala (38) is found dead in her home in the Hollywood Hills. Film credits include – "All That Heaven Allows," "Never Say Goodbye," "Price of Fear," "The Big Boodle," "Don't Go Near the Water," "Battle of the Coral Sea" and "The Guns of Navarone." She was once described as a woman who "looks a little like Ingrid Bergman, a little like Grace Kelly, like Nancy Olson around the eyes and like four or five of those sexy Italian actresses below the neck." She died of an apparent drug overdose. Last July, she was seriously injured when her sports car overturned on a winding road in the Hollywood Hills.

Below Gia's notice was the obituary of the actor Bruce Cabot, who died at 68 years of age. While he had appeared in more than 300 pictures, including the classic 1933 film "King Kong," with such a significant Filmography the newspaper gave him ten words, but my sister with seventeen film credits was allocated 111 words. However, J. Edgar Hoover's death notice eclipsed everyone. The May 2nd front page of the "Los Angeles Times" covered the story of his life and accomplishments, but so did all the newspapers in the country.

My sister's funeral was held during the morning of Thursday May 4th; that day anyone reading Joyce Haber's entertainment column in the "Los Angeles Times" would not have read about Gia, instead Joyce shocked her readers when she wrote that the squeaky clean teenybopper singer David Cassidy of "The Partridge Family" fame was to appear bare-chested on the cover and nude in the centerfold of "Rolling Stone."

On the morning of my sister's funeral Dore and I were driven to Saint Victor's Church in West Hollywood. A stately modern structure located a block behind Sunset Boulevard not far from the "Whiskey a Go-go," and walking distance to the "Classic Cat" -- known as the swankest striptease club in the city. While the church was the parish of such great and dignified films stars as Irene Dunne and Loretta Young, Sunset Strip was the cathedral of action.

Outside the church we saw reporters, press photographers, television reporters and cameramen. Waiting for an opportunity to photograph and or interview the celebrities who came to pay their respects. Carefully keeping a vigil of the attendees; meanwhile the curious looky-loos some wearing shorts and tee-shirts added to the circus like atmosphere.

I arrived arm in arm with Dore. As we neared the hoopla in front of the church, I tilted my head towards him, hiding my face behind the wide brim of my black hat. I was avoiding the paparazzi. When we entered the church, an usher immediately spotted us, and took us to the family section that was located to one side of the altar.

Gia's casket was covered with a blanket of red roses, white orchids, delphiniums, maiden hair ferns and red ribbons. The floral tributes were lovely, especially a unique spray of yellow roses. Later I discovered Daniel La Biena, his mother Esther, and Larry Archer sent it. Daniel and Larry were two of Gia's house guests that she had the Police kick-out on the day she died. I questioned the correctness of the floral offering. Symbolically yellow flowers represented a strong tie between the deceased and the sender. What connection did they have with my sister? She got rid of them. For me their tribute was an insult; like a slap on the face with a white glove.

One of Gia's neighbors Joe Bustamante who was an interior designer, along with John Wahllieb and Larry Langston, the latter two were the other house guests my sister had to evict. They sent an enormous vase arrangement of red roses. Their card read: "From your friends and neighbors." I was speechless.

The film director Robert Aldrich and his new wife the fashion model Sybille Siegfried-Aldrich sent a beautiful arrangement. Aldrich divorced Harriet in 1966.

Merrill and Elaine Heatter sent a standing spray of pink and white gladioli, lavender sweet peas, pink tulips, and rose-dyed carnations. Mrs. Heatter before retiring from films was known as Elaine Stewart, an actress, somewhat of a sex - symbol that MGM had groomed to compete with Twentieth – Century Fox's Marilyn Monroe. Her husband was a screenwriter and producer who for twenty years had collaborated with Bob Quigley in Heatter-Quigley Productions, famous for the TV shows "Hollywood Squares," and "Gambit."

"May heaven light your way," wrote Shelly Winters on a card that was attached to the lovely arrangement of pink gladioli and white carnations.

Following the mass, the attendees lined up to visit Gia. After they saw her, they came to the family section where I was sitting with Dore. They'd pay their respects, and then walked away.

It's funny the thoughts that run through one's mind at a critical time like this one. In the background I heard the organist play Bach's "Ave Maria," but I couldn't get another song out of my head. It was the "Midnight Cowboy" theme song.

Everybody's talking at me, but I don't hear a word they're saying, only the echoes of my mind....

Then it was time for me to pay my respects to Gia. Dore held my arm as I walked toward the coffin. I stopped and peered in. She didn't look like my sister; she looked like a movie star. Although her auburn hair was nicely combed, but there was so much makeup on her face; she'd been made up to look like she was the star in a Hollywood premiere. Over-glamorized and theatrical, perhaps that was done for the media, the fans who might have sneaked in for a glimpse, or even some of her friends. What was lying in the coffin was not my beautiful, smart, and charming sister; that was not the girl I grew up with in Mili San Marco. I took a flower from a wreath and placed it in the hand of the poor creature. Then I felt as if I was going to become sick, I started to feel dizzy. Dore helped me out of the church.

The funeral cortege was waiting. Dore took me to the family car, he opened the door, I got in and he sat next to me. I watched the pallbearers put the coffin into the hearse then close the door. I could see the casket through the windows. Slowly the driver pulled away from the curb; there were six black limousines that followed.

CB

Gia Scala

To Live One Day as a Lion....

More than 40 years ago Gia died. I haven't accepted her death; however, I've learned to live with her absence. Sometimes when I'm sleeping she comes to me in my dreams. Still beautiful, daring, loving, and wonderful; then like bubbles in Champagne, Poof! She's gone, and I awake.

In 1972, there was much to do after she left. Her paintings were important to her. During her lifetime she completed 30 canvases. I remember she had dated Pearce Young. He was an art patron and the vice chair of the California Arts Commission. She mentioned to me that he appreciated her art work, and believed she had a future as a painter. I remembered she told me his day job was that of a judge at the Los Angeles Superior Court. When I called to ask what I should do with Gia's paintings, he said he'd pick them up and have them framed.

Afterwards, he invited me to dinner at his home. When I walked in I saw my sister's paintings beautifully framed and hanging on his walls. They looked wonderful. Later, he would donate them to the Arts Commission.

Gia had a beautiful portrait of herself that a well known artist painted. I gave it to Dore. He had a tremendous collection of photographs, memorabilia, and paintings not only of Joan Crawford, but many actors and actresses.

The furniture that remained in her house, I sold, or else found a home for it. I kept her scrap books, studio and personal photographs, and some of her gowns. These items I treasure; especially her dresses. After she died, when I missed her, and was feeling I wanted to talk to her, or be with her, I'd put on one of her gowns. It felt as if she were embracing me. As time passed, I let that go and put them away.

Sally Kellerman bought her home. I've never returned to that house. Looking back, how strange that Gia's possessions seemed to go where they were meant to be.

The probate court took two years to settle her estate. When it did, I received some money. With it I bought a four-plex in Hollywood. I resided in one of the apartments and rented the other three.

Hollywood became my home. During my time in the City, I've participated in community events such as "The Mannequins Association" and have helped the L.A. Juvenile

Hall with philanthropic work. The Hollywood Chamber of Commerce nominated me for Princess of Hollywood.

I continued acting, and have been in movies, commercials, and have appeared on Television shows. However, my favorite activity was the theater. In memory of my sister I founded "The Scala Repertory Company." The first production was of Joe Orton's comedy entitled "Loot."

Looking back at Gia's life, I realize she had a full life of excitement, fun, drama, and oh yes, love: Her fans adored her; wherever she went she was applauded, and through the magic of the movies new generations will know her.

On a personal level, she loved a man with all her heart, and he loved her back. Although he left, it was part of her karma.

I've come to recognize that Gia wasn't meant to be among us for a long time, but while she was here, she had one heck of a good time.

From the time she was born until the time she died, nothing was common about her. Sometimes I become melancholy because she had a short life, but then I take comfort in our Father's proverb. "Girls," he would say, "It is better to live one day as a lion than ten years as a sheep."

ᘓᙠ

Tina's Photo Album

Life in Hollywood

When I met Bob Hope he asked me, "Are you in the Mafia?"

Shelly Winters and me. She became my friend and acting teacher.

Patrick Swayze and me at the Golden Apple Awards

I played Mrs. Torrio in "Capone" starring Harry Guardino as Johnny Torrio

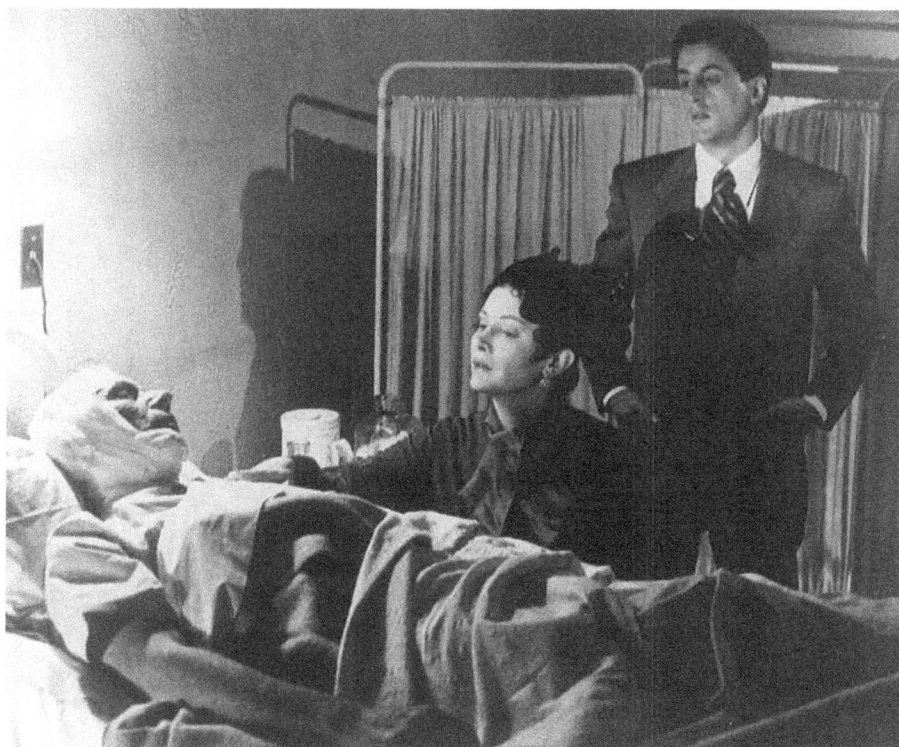

Harry Guardino, in the hospital bed, me as Mrs. Torrio and Sylvester Stallone, standing behind me who played Frank Nitti, in the 1975 movie "Capone."

Above: "A Cavalcade of Style" fashion show for the benefit of C.A.R.E.S. held at the Queen Mary in Long Beach, California. Lee Meriwether standing next to me.

Iron Eyes Cody and me, I wrote a song about him

Merv Griffin and me....

with Ray Bradbury

Me, Debbie Reynolds, and the restaurateur Emilio Baglioni

Above: Linda Crystal sitting next to me

Tommy Smothers, me and Emilio Baglioni

With President and Mrs. Reagan

In the middle is Miss Germany 1975, Marina Langer, and Zsa Zsa Gabor right

Modeling for a social affair

Glam, Glam, Glam!

At Movie Land Wax Museum with Gia's wax figure; the scene is from the "The Guns of Navarone.

ଔ

Filmography

Gia Scala

1964: Operation Delilah
Sidney W. Pink Productions

1962: Il trionfo di Robin
Hood
Buona Vista, Triglav Film

1961: The Guns of
Navarone
Carl Forman Productions

1960: I Aim at the Stars
Morningside Productions

1959: Battle of the Coral
Sea
Morningside Productions

1959: The Angry Hills
Raymond Productions

1958: The Two-Headed Spy
Sabre Film Productions

1958: The Tunnel of Love
Arwin Productions

1958: Ride a Crooked Trail
Universal International
1957: Don't Go Near the
Water
MGM

1957: Tip on a Dead Jockey
MGM

1957: The Garment Jungle
Columbia

1957: The Big Boodle
Monteflor Productions

1957   Four Girls in Town
Universal International

1956: The Price of Fear
Universal International

1956: Never Say Goodbye
Universal International

1955: All that Heaven
Allows
Universal International

Television

1969: It Takes a Thief
"The Artist is for Framing"
Angel

1969: The Name of the
Game
"The Inquiry"
Renata Marino

1967: Tarzan
"The Golden Runaway"
Martha Tolboth

1966: Jericho
"Upbeat & Underground"
Simone DuBray

1965: Run for Your Life
"How to Sell Your Soul for
Fun & Profit"
Marika Takacs

1965: 12 O'Clock High
"R/X for a Sick Bird"
Ilka Zradna

1965: Voyage to the
Bottom of the Sea
"Jonah & the Whale"
Dr. Katya Markova

1965: Convoy
"Passage to Liverpool"
Madeline Duval

1965: The Rogues
"The Laughing Lady of
Luxor"
Lisa de Montfort

1964: The Rogues
"Take Me to Paris"
Simone Carnot

1964: The Alfred Hitchcock
Hour
"The Sign of Satan"
Kitty Frazier

1961: Alfred Hitchcock
Presents
"Deathmate"
Lisa Talbot

1961: Hong Kong
"The Runaway"
Maria Banda

1961: Here's Hollywood
Episode: 1.154
Herself

1960: The Islanders
"Duel of Strangers"
Rhea

1960: Alfred Hitchcock
Presents
"Mother, May I Go Out to
Swim?"
Lottie Rank

1957: Goodyear Theater
"A London Affair"
Giovanna

C3

Gia Scala

Index

Abner Biberman
    director *The Price of Fear*,
    157
Academy Award, 252
Adolf Hitler
    Hitler recognized an
        opportunity to seize
        the Suez Canal, 51
    Mussolini aligns with
        Hitler, 31
    Mussolini supported
        Hitler's rise to power,
        50
    sent General Rommel, 51
Adolphe Menjou, 140
Agnes Moorehead, 151
Al Jolson, 155
Alfred Hitchcock
    Spellbound, 248
Algonquin Hotel, 260
Alistair MacLean
    author of *The Guns of
    Navarone*, 245
Allied Control Commission,
    66

letter recommending
    Father, 67
Allied forces, 54, 55, 63, 64,
    66, 70
Anna Kashfi, 181, 293, 294
Anne Francis, 181
Anthony Quayle, 8
Arnold Rothstein
    bootlegger, 168
Arthur Lowe, Jr., 217
Audie Murphy, 198
Aunt Agata, 102, 103
    a religious home, 160
    marries Angelo Puglisi,
    116
Aunt Julia, 137
    becomes a widow, 137
    Bethel, Connecticut, 272
    Black Irish, 272
    embarrasses Kate, 274
    has a stroke, 277
    has lunch in New York
        with Tina & Kate, 273
    moves to New York, 196
    takes a little nip, now &
        then, 273

with shotgun, 272

Aunt Lizzy, 78, 89, 198
  Gia's Godmother, 86

Baron Francis Von Kahler, 128

Benito Mussolini, 31
  His Fascist government in collusion with Mafiosi, 31

Bert Parks
  TV show host, 139

Betty Boop, 192

Bill Todman
  TV Show producer with Mark Goodson, 139

Billboard, 268, 269

Brown Derby Restaurant, 291

Bruce Cabot
  starred in 1933 film *King Kong*, 307

Buddy Ebsen, 234

Bugsy Siegel, 168

Senator John Downey Works, 119

Camay Records
  auditioning for new talent, 267
  Don Ames and Hal Weiss, founders of, 269

Captain Kelly, 73, 75, 92
  The Heron, Captian of, 99
  Tina & Mother sail on *The Heron* for London, 126

Carl Foreman
  screenwriter, *The Guns of Navarone*, 245

Carlo Menotti, famous voice coach
  Judy Garland, Harry Belafonte, Tony Bennett, Bobby Darin, former students, 262

Carlos Rivas
  actor in *The Big Boodle*, 163

Carmella, 112, 113, 115
  Father's sister who had died young, 36

Carroll O'Connor, 299

Cary Grant, 144

Central Park, 138, 265, 274

Cesare Mori, 31

Charles Drake, 157

Charles Simonelli
  film executive, 217

Charlton Heston, 202

Christa Lang, 283

Clint Eastwood, 287
  Maggie, wife of, 287
  Pebble Beach Celebrity Tennis Tournament, 287
  played lab assistant Will in *Never Say Goodbye*, 151
  spaghetti western, 257
  Universal contract player, 147

Conte Grande, 121

Cornelius Sullivan
 farmer, father of 11
  children, passed away
  in 1924, 196
 Gia & Tina's Irish
  grandfather, 195
Crete König Albert, 121
Cuba
 Filming location for *The
  Big Boodle*, 161
Curt Jürgens
 played the part of Dr.
  Wernher von Braum,
  241
Daniel La Biena
 handyman?, 297
 invited 3 of his friends to
  move into Gia's home,
  296
 meets Gia, 296
 reported Gia's death to
  the Police, 8
 returned after he was
  kicked out, 297
 sent yellow flowers to
  Gia's funeral, 309
David Cassidy
 appeared in *Rolling Stone*
  centerfold, 308
Dean Cornwell
 fine arts painter
  decorated the dining
  room at The Warwick,
  138
Dick Tracy, 270
Dillon Smith

becomes Tina's husband,
 129
Dillon Sr, 131
Don Burnett, 187, 188, 218,
 221, 231, 251
 Barbara Anderson, 2nd
  wife of, 286
 considered a Rock
  Hudson look a-like,
  187
 Damon & Pythias co-
  starred, 258
 dates actress Lori Nelson,
  188
 Gia became smitten, 16
 Gia's husband to be, 151
 Northwest Passage, 221,
  234
 pallbearer at Gia's funeral,
  305
 photo, 218
 played Robin Hood, 256
 starred in TV show
  Northwest Passage, 11
 Wedding photo Gia &
  Steve McQueen, 135
Dore Freeman, 178
 1st time sees Joan
  Crawford, 179
 admired Hurrell's
  photographs, 180
 begins at MGM, 179
 dead 1988, 181
 helped Tina with Gia's
  funeral arrangements,
  306

helps Crawford, 179
meets Gia, 181
MGM publicist, 175
photo with Tina, 187
president of Joan
    Crawford's Fan Club,
    178
sees Greta Garbo in NY,
    178
told Gia & Tina their
    Mother passed away,
    199
Doris Day, 202, 206, 239
Dorothy Kingsley
    screen writer, *Don't Go
    Near the Water*, 305
Dorothy Malone, 189
Douglas Fairbanks, Jr
    actor & Joan Crawford's
    husband, 179
Douglas Sirk
    director Gia's 1st movie,
    145
Dr. Wernher von Braum,
    241
Duke Goldstone, 270
Dustin Hoffman
    as Ratso, 276
Earl Holliman, 183
Earl Wilson
    show biz columnist
        announced Tina cast in
        Seconds, movie
        starring Rock Hudson,
        267
Eartha Kitt, 217

Eileen O'Sullivan - Scoglio
    behind enemy lines, 49
    diagnosed with lung
        cancer, 172
    has a few months to live,
        193
    in the cave, 62
    our Mother, 20
    photo with Gia, 200
    received letter from
        neighbor, 88
    surrounded by Nazi
        soldiers, 57
Elaine Stewart, former
    actress, somewhat of a
    sex symbol, 310
Ernest Hemingway
    owned a ranch " la finca"
    in Cuba, 167
Ernest Hemmingway
    Old Man and the Sea,
    153
Errol Flynn, 157
    autobiography, *My
    Wicked, Wicked Ways*,
    172
    Don Juan, 158
    Flynn's father, Professor
        Theodore Thompson
        Flynn, 171
    General George
        Armstrong Custer, 158
    Jim Corbett, 158
    offered his schooner the
        Zaca to Gia, 172
    Robin Hood, 158

Erskine Johnson
   Hollywood gossip
      columnist, 248
Eva Gabor, 181
Fidel Castro, 166
Franchot Tone, 179
Frank Gorshin, 140
Frankie Carle, 268
Fulgencio Batista, 163
Gene Kelly, 14, 203
General Eisenhower, 52
General Montgomery, 51
   in Messina, Sicily, 69
General Omar Bradley, 64
General Rommel, 51
George Hurrell
   famous Hollywood
      photographer, 180
   plein-air artist colony in
      Laguna Beach, Calif.,
      180
George M. Cohan
   Yankee Doodle Dandy,
      117
George Nader, 191
George Raft
   actor who became
      meeter & greeter at
      Cuban casino, 167
Gia
   aka Giovanna Scoglio,
      139
   All That Heaven Allows,
      145
   auditioned for the film
      The Galileans, 140

becomes beauty queen
   aboard *SS Vulcania*,
   102
Beirgarten table, gift
   from Curt Jürgens, 243
car accident on
   Muholland Drive, 291
Church Confirmation in
   Ireland, 87
complains about living
   with Aunt Agata, 128
contract with Universal
   International, 145
discovered on *Stop the
   Music*, 139
filed for divorce, 280
Gia & Don, wedding
   photos, 223
goes to Paris, 280
ingested the drug
   Ketamine, 293
lived with Aunt Agata in
   Whitestone, NY, 111
makes 1st screen test
   with actor Ray Danton,
   141
met Marlon Brando, 294
name at birth Josephine
   Grace Johanna Scoglio-
   O'Sullivan, 35
Never Say Goodbye, Gia's
   2nd film, 151
photo at Pier Angeli's
   Baby Shower, 149
photo sailing on Flynn's
   Zaca, 174

photo with Errol Flynn, 162

photo with Henry Miller & Christa Lang, 284

put under psychiatric observation, 293

rear-ended Don's 1957 Cadillac Coupe Deville, 278

released under Anna Kashfi's care, 294

riding horses in Ireland, 79

suspicion of battery, 292

Sybil Brand Institution, 292

takes acting classes from Stella Adler, 130

The Big Boodle movie with Errol Flynn, 193

the men evicted on the day she died Daniel La Biena John Wahllied, Larry Langston, & Larry Archer, 309

The Price of Fear, 157

visited Ireland in 1970, 89

Gia 1st starring film *Don't Go Near the Water*, 175

Gibraltar, 76

Gig Young, 13, 14, 203 Elaine Young, wife of, 13

Giuseppe Garibaldi with a 1,000 man expedition overturned the Kingdom of the Two Sicily's, 24

Glenn Ford, 175

Gloria Swanson, 178, 249

Greenwich Village, 26

Gregory Peck, 244, 251 wants Gia to play the part of Anna, 245

Greta Garbo, 178

Guy Williams, 297 Gia death benefits went to, 10 Janice Cooper, wife of, 259 starred in *Damon & Pythias*, 259 well known for *Lost in Space* and *Zorro*, 259

Harry Cohn President of Columbia Pictures, 192

Hedda Hopper, 188, 208, 218, 226, 244, 255, 257

Henry Mancini, 191 photo with Gia, 202 visited Gia, 201

Henry Miller, 6, 9, 281 Geraldine Fitzgerald, Hildegard Knef, Ziva Rodann, Ava Gardner, Kim Novak, Diane Baker, Inger Stevens, & Gia, 282

Hoki Tokuda, wife of, 281
postcard to Gia, 281
Her Majesty Queen Elizabeth II, 252
Hollywood Star System, 143
Ingrid Bergman, 248
Institute of Saint Anna
  Irish nuns more lenient than the Sicilian nuns, 83
Institute of Saint Anna
  Mother Superior, very short Sicilian nun who ruled the Institute with an iron fist in a velvet glove, 42
  Nuns fainted during class at, 39
  Our first school, 39
Irene Dunne, 308
Irish Grandmother
  baking Irish soda bread over an open fire, 78
  Johanna Shagrue-Sullivan, 78
Irving Thalberg, 181
J. Edgar Hoover
  obituary, 307
J. Lee Thompson
  film director, *The Guns of Navarone*, 251
Jack Hawkins
  The Two Headed Spy, 210

Jack Kerouac, 153
Jack Lord, 189
Jack Warner
  gives the boot to Errol Flynn, 159
Jane Wyman, 151
Jean Harlow, 178
Jeanne Crain, 157
Jerry Hopper
  film director, *Never Say Goodbye*, 151
Joan Crawford, 144
  Dore Freeman adored, 178
John Frankenheimer
  director, *Seconds*, 267
John Gavin, 191
Joyce Haber
Julie Adams, 191
Kate Sullivan
  Aunt Kate, 136
  Aunt Kate's high society friend, 80
  helped Tina with her apartment, 264
  invited Tina to New York, 260
  returns to Ireland, 277
Keenan Wynn, 188
Keith Larsen, 234
Kenmare, 83, 84, 85, 88, 195
King Ferdinand II, 24
Kingdom of the Two Sicily's, 24
La Limonaria, 34, 51, 63

export company, 30
shipping important for
    success, 31
Lana Turner, 142
Larry Langston, 8
Lawrence Welk, 268
Lee J. Cobb, 192
Lemon Trust of Palermo,
    120
Leslie Nielson, 218
Lex Barker, 157
Lili Kardell
    Universal contract player,
    148
Liverpool, 31, 34, 77, 99
Lock Ness, 81
Loretta Young, 308
Lori Nelson, 188
Louella Parsons
    gossips about Errol Flynn
    & Gia, 160
    Mrs. Agatha Smith
    arrives from London,
    195
Louis D. Snader, 269
Louis G. Cowan
    Quiz show creator, 139
Mafiosi, 31, 50
Marilyn Monroe
    Blonde Bombshell image,
    142
Marion Davis
    The Warwick her pied-à-
    terre, 138
Mark Goodson
    TV show producer, 139

Marlon Brando
    Christian, son of, 294
Marshal family, 127
Martin Melcher
    Doris Day's husband, 203
Mary F. Tobin
    from Irish background,
    immigrates to New
    York, 121
    wife of Pietro Scoglio, 26
Mary Sullivan
    Gia & Tina's great
    grandmother, 196
Maurice Bergman, 140
    accepted position with
    Motion Picture
    Association of America,
    156
Merle Oberon, 157
Merv Griffin, 288
Meyer Lansky
    American Gangster, 167
Mili Marina, 61, 73, 109,
    111, 126
Mili San Marco, 24, 35, 49,
    51, 56, 73, 99, 105, 108,
    111, 112, 113, 115, 116
    cave in the hills, 50
Model Drug Dealer Liability
    Act, 299
Motion Picture Association
    of America, 156
Nat "King" Cole, 267
Natale Scoglio
    clever capitalist, 114
    export business, 114

Grandfather, 20

Grazia Sfravara, 1st wife of, 24

Letteria Sangiorgio 2nd wife of, 113

older brother Pasquale Scoglio, 114

one of the biggest lemon producers in Messina, 29

returns to Mili San Marco after 2nd wife dies, 116

Trademark for combustible motorcar engine, 112

National Italian Democratic League, 119

Nazi, 51, 54, 55, 57, 58, 61, 62, 241

New York Fruit Exchange, 26

Norma Shearer, 178, 181

Olivia De Havilland, 158

Operation Husky, 52

Oscar W. Underwood

supports Sicilian imported lemons, 119

Paramount, 140

Payne-Aldrich Tariff

applied to imported lemons, 118

Peer Oppenheimer

director, author, screenplay writer, 238

Peggy Lee, 267

Pérez Prado

Cuban pianist & band leader, 165

Pier Angeli

expecting 1st child, 148

Pietro Scoglio

asked his daughters if they would like to visit their Irish Grandmother, 75

becomes political within the Italian New York community, 120

earns large amount of money in New York, 118

Father, 10

Father, 20

Father came for us, 63

fired all the servants, 88

friends with General Montgomery, 69

married Eileen O'Sullivan, 197

married Mary F. Tobin, 121

New York Fruit Exchange, 118

Sicilian lemon importer, 118

Pietro Scoglio half sister Angela

Pietro Scoglio's half brother Salvatore

Pietro Scoglio's half sister Serafina

Pietro Scoglio's half sister

Concetta Grazia Scoglio, 113

Pio Parolin
parish Priest who married Pietro Scoglio and Mary Tobin, 27

Plato Skouras
Spyros Skouras' son, 210

Poncho Barnes
female flying ace, 180

Purslane, 55, 56

Queen Elizabeth
Trans-Atlantic passenger ship, 202

Ramón Novarro
star of silent movies, 181

Richard Boone,, 192

Richard Burton, 157

Richard Thorpe
director, *Tip on a Dead Jockey*, 189

Richard Widmark, 203
photo with Gia, 204

Ring of Kerry, 77

Robert Aldrich, 192, 213, 226, 227, 309

Robert Mitchum, 210, 213
photo with Gia, 212
The Angry Hills, 211

Robert Taylor, 189

Rock Hudson
becomes the perfect man image, 142
born Roy Harold Scherer, Jr., 144

Don Burnett lives with, 278

early gossip about, 220

meets Mother, 145

Never Say Goodbye, 151

photo with Gia & Mother, 146

Phyllis Gates, wife of, 220

starred in *All That Heaven Allows*, 145

starred in sci-fi flick *Seconds*, 267

with Gia & Don Burnett, 238

Rod Taylor, 220, 221

Rosa Cucircotta
Godmother, 46

Russ Tamblyn, 230

Sally Kellerman, 280
bought Gia's home, 13

Samson Burke
actor & bodybuilder, 258

Samuel Fuller, 283

Sandra Dee, 140

Sardinia, 148

Scaletta, 61

Senator John Downey Works, 119

Sergio Leone, 257

Shelly Winters, 310, 317

Sicilian communists, 50

Sicilian Grandmother
Grazia Sfravara, 24
Passed away, 111

Spyros Skouras

President Century-Fox
introduced
Cinemascope, 157
SS König Albert
cargo / passenger ship,
114
SS Vulcania, 103, 121, 122
photo of, 122
sailed to New York, 100
Stella Adler, 129
Steve McQueen, 16, 230,
231
meets Mother, 138
Neile Adams, wife of, 231
photo at Gia's wedding,
135
wants to marry Gia, 134
Stop the Music, 139
Tahilla, 34, 77, 136, 195,
196
Taormina, Sicily
Father's retirement, 214
Telescriptions, 269, 270
Uncle Denie, 81
Terry Kingsley
actor & screenwriter, 305
The Guns of Navarone, 8,
244, 251, 254, 334
Anthony Quinn, David
Niven, Stanley Baker,
Anthony Quayle,
James Darren, Irene
Papas, 245
The Liberace Show, 270
The Warwick, 137
Thomas Noguchi

Marilyn Monroe, 298
Tina Scala
Actor's Studio, student of,
262
Bikini Photo, 109
Capone, 1975 film, 320
Fifi Oscard's talent
agency, 264
film debut in *Seconds*,
267
Gia writes to Tina, 101
in Ireland saves Gia's life
1st time, 82
James Garner, 288
Jon Voight, was flirty
with, 276
Loveable Lingerie, 264
Marie Pigalle Makeup,
265
McFadden Bartell, 264
Merv Griffin, 288
Midnight Cowboy, 276
Midnight Cowboy theme
song, 310
Morton Lazarus, to marry,
265
photo goes viral, 266
Princess of Hollywood,
315
received fan mail, 266
saves Gia's life 2nd time,
288
US GIs' decide to make
Tina their new pinup
girl, 266

Walter Winchell reports, 265

with Aunt Kate, 275

Tommy Burns

World's Heavyweight Champ, 117

Tommy Dorsey

recorded "Cha Cha Cha for Gia, 191

Uncle Denie, 78, 80, 82, 89

Gia's Godfather, 86

Universal

changed Gia's name, 123

Universal International, 140

Universal International meets Peter Johnson, 141

Vic Damone

married to Pier Angeli, 148

Victor Mature, 157

Vincent Sherman

director replaced Aldrich in *Garment Jungle*, 193

Walter Winchell, 188

column announces Tina to marry Lazarus Morton of Calais Originals, 265

William Ramage

described Gia as childlike in some ways, 235

male model & Gia's friend, 183

William Randolph Hearst

built the Warwick, 138

Zaca, 169, 170, 172, 173

Errol Flynn's schooner, 167

photo of bedroom, 170

www.ingramcontent.com/pod-product-compliance
Lightning Source LLC
LaVergne TN
LVHW051450080426
835509LV00017B/1722